CW01511920

# Shakespea. . ....

# The Welsh

Frederick J. Harries

# Alpha Editions

This edition published in 2019

ISBN : 9789353608835

Design and Setting By
**Alpha Editions**
email - alphaedis@gmail.com

# SHAKESPEARE AND THE WELSH

# SHAKESPEARE'S WORKMANSHIP

By Sir Arthur Quiller-Couch, M.A., Litt.D.,
King Edward VII. Professor of English Literature
in the University of Cambridge.    Demy 8vo.,
cloth, 15s. net.                (Third Impression.)

¶ These studies seek to discover, in some of his
plays, just what Shakespeare was trying to do as
a playwright. This has always seemed to the
author a sensible way of approaching him, and
one worth reverting to from time to time. For
it is no disparagement to the erudition and scholarship that have so piously been heaped about
Shakespeare to say that we shall sometimes find
it salutary to disengage our minds from it all, and
recollect that the poet was a playwright. In thus
considering some of Shakespeare's chief plays as
pieces of workmanship (or artistry) the book
follows a new road that is all the better worth
trial because it lies off the trodden way.

T. FISHER UNWIN, LTD., LONDON

# SHAKESPEARE
## AND
# THE WELSH

BY

FREDERICK J. HARRIES

T. FISHER UNWIN, LTD.
LONDON: ADELPHI TERRACE

FIRST PUBLISHED IN 1919

English Alumnus

# INTRODUCTION

For the Welsh people everywhere the works of Shakespeare should possess a peculiar interest. Shakespeare, as these pages will disclose, knew the Welsh, if he did not know Wales; for in Stratford-on-Avon there existed, in his time, a veritable Welsh colony, and there is reason to think that he may have been on terms of the closest intimacy with more than one of its members. As a result, he has given us some notable portraits of the typical Welshman of his period. But not only was Shakespeare familiar with Welsh society; it seems reasonably proved that he had Welsh blood in his veins, and it may have been from the lips of a Welsh grandmother that he obtained his first knowledge of Welsh tradition and folklore, which, as we shall hope to show, exerted no small influence upon his dramatic and lyrical genius.

In his analysis of the Welsh character Shakespeare found much to praise, and a singularly friendly attitude toward the Welsh nation is revealed by his introduction in *King Henry V.* of a scene in which a Welsh captain makes an

5

English braggart " eat the leek "—a scene very possibly intended to put an end to ridicule of the Welsh.

There are many Celtic elements in Shakespeare's plays. The motives of two of his greatest tragedies, *Macbeth* and *King Lear*, were drawn from the old Celtic chronicles, and a portion of the plot of *Cymbeline* was taken from the same source. Indeed, a general survey of the Celtic elements and their expression in Shakespeare's works will afford us many striking pictures of the legendary and historic past of the Celtic race. With Lear we move among the barbaric splendours and elemental passions of a Britain " when Joash was King of Judah "; we gaze across the battle-field from the tent of Cymbeline to descry the golden eagle of Augustus Cæsar flashing in the sun; with Glendower we live again amid the turmoil of the fierce but futile struggle for Cymric liberty and independence; with Fluellen we witness upon the field of Agincourt the triumph of a " Welsh King " who was one of the " goot men porn at Monmouth"; with patriotic pride we follow the grandson of Owen ap Meredith ap Tudor through conspiracies and deadly conflicts to that serener summit from which we are able to behold the vision of a great and glorious Empire; and, lastly, with Sir Hugh

6

Evans we leave the treachery and splendour of Courts, the roll of drum, and call of trumpet, for the genial company of the middle-class English citizens of Tudor times, partaking of their hospitality and joining in their revels. Thus " in motion of no less celerity than that of thought " we fly from scene to scene, while prince and courtier, cardinal and archbishop, earl and knight, priest and physician, soothsayer and cowled monk, gallant and bravo, minstrel and jester, pass and repass before us, against a background of frowning castles, serried battlements, loopholed gateways, stately fanes, ancestral halls, bustling, slipshod inns, and the high-gabled, timber-framed dwelling-houses that line the narrow, cobbled streets.

For the benefit of the English reader it may be explained that the name Welsh was originally applied by the Teutons of Britain and the Continent to all whom they regarded as foreigners or strangers; hence the Celts of Britain were known to them as " Welsh."

In modern German *welsch* signifies French or Italian, also foreign, outlandish; *welscher* is an Italian, a Frenchman; while *wälschen* or *welschen* means " to gibber, to speak gibberish."

" No Welshman now," says Thomas Stephens, the author of *The Literature of the Kymry*, "ever

7

thinks of resenting the appellation. If the term Welsh ever had any sting in it, it has long been taken out, and so far from being a term of reproach is a name in which a million Welsh-speaking Welshmen [there are many more to-day] take a favourable pride, and a name which happily stands for some of the noblest elements in the life of the British people throughout the Empire."

FREDERICK J. HARRIES.

# CONTENTS

# SHAKESPEARE AND THE WELSH

## CHAPTER I

### STRATFORD-ON-AVON—THE WELSH SCHOOLMASTER

SHAKESPEARE was born at Stratford-on-Avon in the month of April, 1564, and he died in the same town on April 23rd, 1616. It is believed that his death occurred on the fifty-second anniversary of his birth, but there is no positive evidence of the precise date of the latter event, the only entry in the parish register being that of his baptism, on April 26th, 1564.

It is proved that a considerable number of Welshmen were settled in Stratford-on-Avon during the years of Shakespeare's youth. Among the names appearing in the town's records are those of Ap Roberts, Ap Rice, Ap Williams, Ap Edwards, Hugh ap Shon, Howel ap Howell, Evans Rice, Evans Meredith, and others. The middle classes had not yet learned to shut themselves jealously in their houses, each man suspicious of his neighbour's morals or manners; there was plenty of

13

genial intercourse between fellow-citizens in the market-place, the council-chamber, the churchyard, and the tavern. Such intercourse is not wholly dead in the market towns of the present day; in a town as small as Stratford (whose population could not have been much greater than 2,000), it was one of the conditions of daily life. Apart from daily propinquity, it is likely that the English inhabitants, young and old, would have felt a certain curiosity regarding people rejoicing in such odd patronymics, many of whom would have spoken the English language with a very marked and very " foreign " accent. Shakespeare's intercourse with the Welsh, however, was not merely of a casual nature. Aubrey discovered that he had, as a young man, a warm affection for a boy, some years his junior, the son of Griffin ap Roberts, a butcher.

The " small Latin and less Greek " which Ben Jonson ascribed to his " Swan of Avon " were acquired at the Stratford-on-Avon Grammar School, which was revived by the charter of Edward VI., in 1555, and was for a time held in the Guild Chapel. Shakespeare, according to the best authorities, attended this school from his seventh until his thirteenth year. He was then, apparently, withdrawn to assist his father in his business of glover, wool stapler, purveyor of agricultural produce, and possibly butcher. His first schoolmaster was Walter Roche, B.A., Fellow of Corpus Christi College, but Roche was on the point of retiring when Shakespeare entered the school. The new headmaster was Simon Hunt, afterwards curate of Luddington. There is a tradition that Shakespeare and Anne Hathaway were married in that village. Simon Hunt's term of office appears to have ended about the year 1577, when the master's chair was filled by one Thomas Jenkins, a Welshman, who was a Master of Arts of St. John's College, Oxford. These headmasters were appointed by the Council, but were licensed to preach by the Bishop of Worcester. There is no record to show that Shakespeare received any portion of his schooling under Thomas Jenkins—he may have left school before Thomas Jenkins was installed; but we may reasonably suppose that he was interested in the change of headmastership, and, as we shall presently see, it is probable that at a later period he came into daily contact with the Welsh scholar.

John Aubrey, Shakespeare's earliest biographer, tells us that when William Shakespeare was a boy he exercised his father's trade, and " when he killed a calfe would doe it in high style and make a speech "—which may be history or an amiable

15

legend. He further states that the boy had early a love of poetry and the drama. It is the way of headmasters to " keep an eye " upon promising pupils who have left school, and it is not unreasonable to assume that Shakespeare, as a lad of exceptional parts, would, even as an ex-pupil, have attracted the special attention of Thomas Jenkins.

As an only son he would, for a time, have remained the playfellow of the Grammar School boys, so that he may have had many opportunities of personal intercourse with the good old dominie, and with the insatiable curiosity of genius he may well have plied him with questions concerning the native country of the Pistolian " mountain foreigners " and " mountain squires " who, as residents and visitors, were a feature of Stratford society. And Thomas Jenkins, as a patriotic Welshman, would doubtless have seized the opportunity to impress his youthful questioner with accounts of the musical aptitude, the poetical leanings, the religious fervour, and the indomitable courage of his countrymen. But we have more than this to go upon. Shakespeare, according to local tradition, was for a time second master, or usher, in the Grammar School—a likely enough position for any unusually intelligent pupil who was desirous of continuing his education beyond the tender age of thirteen—and it is a fact that the desk which was sacred to the second master of Stratford Grammar School has always been known as " Shakespeare's desk." So authentic did this tradition seem that the Corporation presented the desk to the Shakespeare birthplace, and there it is to-day.* If we suppose Thomas Jenkins to have been the prototype of Sir Hugh Evans in the *Merry Wives of Windsor* (and this view is adopted by many Shakespearian scholars), then the scene in which Mistress Page questions the Welsh parson-schoolmaster as to the progress at school of her son William assumes a special significance as a reminiscence of the poet's boyhood or ushership. Reading Thomas Jenkins for Sir Hugh Evans in the following passage from the play, we have the picture of a Welsh schoolmaster putting some blockish schoolfellow of the youthful poet through his accidence :

### ACT IV.

#### Scene i.—*The Street.*

*Mrs. Page.* Sir Hugh, my husband says my son profits nothing in the world at his book; I pray you, ask him some questions in his accidence.

*Eva.* Come hither, William; hold up your head; come.

*Mrs. Page.* Come on, sirrah: hold up your head; answer your master, be not afraid.

---

* Yeatman, *The Gentle Shakespeare.*

*Eva.* William, how many numbers is in nouns ?

*Will.* Two.

*Quick.* Truly, I thought there had been one number more; because they say, OD's nouns.

*Eva.* Peace your tattlings.—What is *fair*, William ?

*Will. Pulcher.*

*Quick.* Poulcats ! there are fairer things than poulcats, sure.

*Eva.* You are a very simplicity 'oman; I pray you, peace.—What is *lapis*, William?

*Will.* A stone.

*Eva.* And what is a stone, William ?

*Will.* A pebble.

*Eva.* No, it is *lapis;* I pray you, remember in your prain.

*Will. Lapis.*

*Eva.* That is good, William. What is he, William, that does lend articles ?

*Will.* Articles are borrowed of the pronoun; and be thus declined, *Singulariter, nominativo, hic, hæc, hoc.*

*Eva. Nominativo, hig, hag, hog;*—pray you mark; *genitivo, hujus.* Well, what is your *accusative case ?*

*Will. Accusativo, hinc.*

*Eva.* I pray you, have your remembrance, child; *Accusativo, hing, hang, hog.*

*Quick.* Hang hog is Latin for bacon, I warrant you.

*Eva.* Leave your prabbles, 'oman.

And so it goes on. The result, being unintelligible to her, is apparently satisfactory to Mrs. Page, who at the close of the interrogation remarks: " He is a better scholar than I thought he was;" while Sir Hugh, after the fashion of schoolmasters in the presence of parents, avers that the thickheaded William has " a good sprag memory " (" sprag " for " sprack "—that is, quick, lively).

18

The probability that this scene represents an actual incident from the days of Shakespeare's attendance at the Grammar School, as pupil or master, and therefore the probability that the character of Evans is based upon the said Thomas Jenkins, is increased by the fact that the scene is dragged into the play. It does not advance the action: it is as though the dramatist had a secret affection for Evans, and could not refrain from setting down his reminiscences of Jenkins.

Of Thomas Jenkins we hear nothing further after his departure from Stratford - on - Avon Grammar School.

Before we take our leave, for the present, of Sir Hugh, it may be mentioned that the title " Sir " bestowed upon Sir Hugh Evans, as upon other clergymen in Shakespeare, was equivalent to the French *Sieur* or the Italian *Ser*. It was formerly the common designation of a knight, of one in holy orders, and of a Bachelor of Arts of Cambridge or Dublin; but in the latter instance was always annexed to the surname—as " Sir Evans." For centuries " all the inferior clergy in England were distinguished by this title affixed to the Christian name. Hence our author's Sir Hugh in the present play, Sir Topas in *Twelfth Night*, Sir Oliver in *As You Like It*, etc." (Malone).

19

Mrs. Stopes, in her *Shakespeare's Warwickshire Contemporaries*, gives us a few curious details as to Thomas Jenkins. He became master in 1577, and repairs were made to the schoolhouse for his convenience. An entry dated 1578 shows that the chamberlains " paid to Sir Higges, schoolmaster, 10*l.* [so that Sir Higges would seem to have come between Hunt and Jenkins]; *Item.* To Mr. Jenkins, schoolmaster, his half-year's wages, 10*l.*," the second 10*l.* being paid on January 16th following. In the Wheler Collection is a note by Jenkins to the effect that " John Colby [apparently a mistake for Cotton], late of London, did covenant and agree to give unto me, Thomas Jenkins, in consideration of my departure from the school, the some of 6*l.*" The receipt for this sum bears the date July 9th, 1579, and on July 11th the chamberlain records that he " paid to Mr. Jenkins for Mr. Cotton 6*l.*" In the same year we find, " Paid Mr. Jenkins for his wages, 20*l.*"; so that he appears to have received the full year's wages and a payment of 6*l.*, apparently engaging to remain for two terms.

He was a married man, the Stratford register stating that " Thomas, son to Mr. Thomas Jenkins, was baptised 19 of January, 1577."

We have documentary proof that Shakespeare

used to draw upon his memories of Stratford in naming the characters in his plays. His father, whose adventurous temper led him sadly astray, was in 1592 on the verge of utter ruin. A sensitive man, he shrank from encountering his fellow-townsmen in the days of his adversity. He no longer attended the meetings of the Council, so that after seven years an alderman was elected in his place; and he no longer went to church. Now the law required a monthly attendance; and in this year, 1592, the list of those who failed to attend contained the names of John Shakespeare, Bardolph, and Fluellen, and Hunter tells us that the last two names occurred three years later in the Parish Register.

The lists of " recusants," it is interesting to note, were drawn up by Sir Thomas Lucy of Charlecote Hall. John Shakespeare, it is believed, was inclined to Catholicism; while Lucy, on the other hand, was a hard and uncompromising Puritan, and as one of the commissioners appointed under the statute of 1583, he was invested with a power which would have enabled him to make the lot of the Papists at Stratford-on-Avon anything but pleasant. John Shakespeare's attitude in matters of religion brought him into sharp conflict with the Puritan knight, who certainly could not have been expected to cherish any particular tenderness for a father whose son was believed to have so bitterly lampooned him. There was another reason also for Sir Thomas Lucy's animosity. John Shakespeare, while bailiff of Stratord-on-Avon, had given great encouragement to stage plays, which were anathema to the puritanical mind. William Shakespeare was at the time in London. He did not return to Stratford-on-Avon until 1596, but this date is sufficiently near to that of the list of recusants to justify our supposition that the matter would have been keenly discussed between father and son, and we may guess that it did not increase the poet's affection for Lucy.

In 1597 Shakespeare's two plays dealing with the first and second portions of the reign of Henry IV. were completed, and in the second play we make the acquaintance of Mr. Justice Shallow, whom Falstaff describes as "a man made after supper of a cheese-paring." Mr. Justice Shallow appears again in Shakespeare's next play, *The Merry Wives of Windsor*, which followed closely on *King Henry IV.*, and Sir Thomas Lucy is so mercilessly caricatured in the former play that John Shakespeare and William Fluellen must have felt themselves amply revenged. In Shakespeare's

next work, *King Henry V.*, written in 1598, appears
the character of Fluellen; while Bardolph appears
in no less than four plays. The conjunction of
these two names on the list of recalcitrant church-
goers and in the plays suggests that in seeking
names for his characters, as well as in finding
material for subsidiary scenes, the poet turned
instinctively to his early years in Stratford. During those years it is probable that many Celtic
influences were brought to bear upon him, a circumstance which would explain the considerable
use of Celtic legend and tradition which a close
examination of the plays reveals.

That Shakespeare was familiar with the Welsh
pronunciation of English words is indicated by
the consistent way in which Sir Hugh Evans and
Fluellen drop their initial *w*'s. *W* in Welsh is
pronounced *oo* (as in *woo*), and even to this day
unpolished Welshmen would pronounce woman
as " ooman " and world as " oorld." Such idioms
as " make her a better penny," " there is pippens
and cheese *to come*," and " *make an end* of my
dinner," sound very familiar to Welsh ears. There
is also a Welsh flavour in Sir Hugh's way of using
the noun for the verb or the adjective, as in " can
you affection the 'oman," and " it is a fery des-
cretion answer." The fact that *b* is aspirated

23

in Welsh will account for Fluellen's " Alexander the pig." Again, Sir Hugh Evans tells his fairies to " pinse " Falstaff, because, as a Welshman, he has no digraph to help him over the stile to the English *sh;* while the absence of a *v* in the Welsh alphabet is responsible for Sir Hugh's use of *f* in " fery well." To sum up: whether we consider Shakespeare's knowledge of Welsh character and folklore or the English spoken by the Welsh persons in his plays, we are infallibly led to the conclusion that he knew many Welshmen familiarly and was intimate with some, and that his knowledge was of that deep-seated and instinctive kind which speaks of familiarity in childhood.

# CHAPTER II

## IN LONDON TOWN—THE WAR OF THE THEATRES

WHEN William Shakespeare was eighteen and a half years of age he married Anne Hathaway, and in his twenty-second year he left Stratford-on-Avon for London. Shakespearian authorities used to tell us that his departure was due to his having been concerned in what was then regarded as a legitimate pastime of adventurous and high-spirited youth, a deer-stealing expedition at Charlecote Park, the residence of Sir Thomas Lucy, as a result of which he suffered prosecution at the hands of that gentleman. The story is told by Archdeacon Richard Davies, who was Vicar of Sapperton late in the seventeenth century. It appears that the proceedings against Shakespeare were conducted with a good deal of rancour, which may have been due to religious bigotry or to a previous lampoon; and in revenge for his punishment the poet is said to have penned the famous lines beginning with the words:

> A Parliament member, a justice of Peace,
> At home a Poor Scarecrow, in London an Ass,

and to have affixed them to the park gates of Charlecote Hall. The authority for attributing these lines to Shakespeare was an old man bearing the Welsh name of Thomas Jones, who lived near Stratford-on-Avon and died in 1703 at the age of upwards of ninety years. He had heard the traditional account of the deer-stealing episode from the lips of old inhabitants of Stratford.

Later authorities, however, throw a very different light upon the subject. According to their evidence, it was not in Charlecote Park, but in Falbroke Park that the chasing of the deer took place. Now Falbroke had long been unoccupied— it had, in short, become " disparked "—and the deer within it were under no legal protection. Charlecote lay on the opposite side of the Avon, a little farther down the stream. It is very possible that Sir Thomas Lucy considered himself *ex officio* the custodian of Falbroke, or the deer may have broken cover and taken refuge in Charlecote. Be that as it may, there is reason to believe that Lucy had no good legal pretext for prosecuting the poet; for in *The Merry Wives of Windsor* Justice Shallow, blustering at Falstaff, threatens to make his poaching " a Star Chamber matter," and the Star Chamber was notoriously adapted to trying causes *without reference to the laws of the realm*.

26

How Shakespeare travelled to the Metropolis is a matter of conjecture. The distance from Stratford-on-Avon to London is about 121 miles, and we learn that a pack-horse carrier made the journey at intervals for the purpose of conveying parcels to and fro. Coaches had not yet come into general use, and travellers made their journeys on foot or on horseback. Whatever the manner of his conveyance to London, on his arrival we know that Shakespeare became connected with the theatres, at first in a humble capacity, but later as an actor, and eventually as a reviser and writer of plays.

A detailed description of Shakespeare's progress as a dramatist does not come within the province of this work, but we may mention in passing that when he arrived in the Metropolis one of the companies of licensed actors appearing before the public was under the patronage of Henry Herbert, second Earl of Pembroke, and father of William Herbert, the third Earl, whom some Shakespearian authorities identify with the " W. H." of Shakespeare's *Sonnets.**

The population of London in Shakespeare's time was not more than 300,000, and the population of the whole country was less than that of

See Chapter XIV.

27

London to-day. The Metropolis, in the Elizabethan period, was little better than a country town, but it was then, as it is now, the centre of the political, religious, intellectual, and social activity of England.

The first public theatre erected in England was opened about the middle of Elizabeth's reign, but before the end of it there were no fewer than fifteen playhouses in London alone. Elizabeth, although a lover of the drama, did not attend any of the public theatres—it was not the custom for women to do so—but she witnessed many of the private performances given at her palaces, and Shakespeare appears to have held a high place in the royal favour.

Emerson gives us a glimpse of the poet's early method of work. " At the time," he says, " when Shakespeare left Stratford and went up to London' a great body of stage plays of all dates and writers existed in manuscript, and were in turn produced on the boards. Here is the *Tale of Troy*, which the audience will bear hearing some part of every week; the Death of Julius Cæsar and other stories out of Plutarch, which they will never tire of; a shelf full of English history from the chronicles of Brut and Arthur down to the royal Henrys, which men hear eagerly; and a string of doleful

28

tragedies, merry Italian tales, and Spanish voyages, which all the London prentices know. . . . Shakespeare, in common with his comrades, esteemed the mass of old plays waste stock with which any experiment could be freely tried."

Publication, it must be remembered, was not regarded as an advantage. Printers in search of copy had often to " pirate " successful plays by stealth. They sent a shorthand writer to attend the performances of such plays, or surreptitiously obtained a sight of the manuscript. Plays would usually have been the property of the players, and, if stolen, could be produced by their rivals. Less successful writers might sell their plays to a printer; the more successful frequently postponed publication until the actual or threatened publication of garbled versions led them in self-defence to issue the authentic text.

The theatre in the early days of Elizabeth (says Green) was commonly only the courtyard of an inn, or a mere booth such as is still seen in a country fair. The bulk of the audience sat beneath the open sky in the " pit " or yard; a few covered seats in the galleries which ran round it formed the boxes of the wealthier spectators, while patrons and nobles found seats on the actual boards. All the appliances were of the roughest sort; a few flowers served to indicate a garden, crowds and armies were represented by a dozen scene-shifters with swords and bucklers, heroes rode in and out on hobby-horses, and a scroll on a post told whether the scene was at Athens or London. There were no female actors, and the grossness which startles us in words that fall from women's lips took a different colour when every woman's part was acted by a boy. But difficulties such as these were more than compensated by the popular character of the drama itself. Rude as the theatre might be, all the world was there. The stage was crowded with nobles and courtiers. Apprentices and citizens thronged the benches in the yard below. The rough mob of the pit inspired, as it felt, the vigorous life, the rapid transitions, the passionate energy, the reality, the lifelike medley and confusion, the racy dialogue, the chat, the wit, the pathos, the sublimity, the rant, the buffoonery, the coarse horrors and the vulgar blood-shedding, the immense range over all classes of society, the intimacy with the foulest as well as the fairest developments of human nature which characterised the English stage. The new drama represented " the very age and body of the time, his form and pressure. . . ." Few events in our literary history are so startling as this sudden rise of the Eliza-

30

bethan drama. The rise of the drama led to the building of special theatres. These public play-houses were usually of octagonal or circular shape, and the pit was open to the sky. Under the narrow circular roof there were three galleries, the two lower ones being divided into boxes. The stage ran far into the auditorium. The appliances, as in the case of the improvised theatre of the inn-yard, were, at the outset, of the simplest kind, but as time went on plays were produced with greater elaboration, until in the reign of James curtains and scenic machinery were introduced by Inigo Jones, the famous architect, and after a time the players began to appear in elaborate costumes. Three flourishes on a trumpet an-nounced the beginning of the performance, and a band of musicians supplied the instrumental interludes.

By 1599, when Shakespeare's position was established, he had become a shareholder in the Globe Theatre, drawing at the lowest estimate an income of more than £500 a year, which repre-sented a condition of affluence, since the value of money was then perhaps eight times as great as it is to-day. In 1609 he became a sharer in the profits also of the Blackfriars Theatre, which for many years had been in the possession of a manager bearing the Welsh name of Henry Evans. There is documentary evidence to show that on September 21st, 1600, Henry Evans leased the Blackfriars Theatre from the Burbages, who were the original proprietors, for a term of twenty-one years at a rental of £40 per annum (about £320 in our money); but owing to a breach of covenant on the part of the lessee, who found himself unable to pay the rent, Richard Burbage regained possession of the theatre in 1608. This recovery was obtained as the result of legal proceedings, and in view of the interest of the subject from the Welsh standpoint we give a portion of the petition presented in the course of the proceedings to the Earl of Pembroke, who was then Lord Chamberlain:

" Now for the Blackfriars that is our inheritance; our father purchased it at extreame rates, and made it into a playhouse with great charge and troble which after was leased out to one Evans that first sett up the boyes commonly called the Queene's Majesties Children of the Chappell. In processe of time the boyes growing up to bee men which were Underwood, Field, Ostler, and were taken to strengthen the King's service; and the more to strengthen the service, the boyes dayly wearing out, it was considered that house would bee as fitt for ourselves and soe purchased the lease remaining from Evans with our money and placed men players which were Hemings, Condall, Shakespeare, etc. And Richard Burbage."

To these, in 1610, as well as to the dispossessed lessee, shares in the receipts were granted.

Henry Evans, during his connection with the Blackfriars Theatre, had under his direction a youthful company of actors known as the Children of the Chapel Royal. These boy actors soon became the rage, and a fierce rivalry ensued between the older actors and the youthful new-comers. The leading dramatists (with the exception of Shakespeare) took sides, and satirical exchanges were made through the medium of the plays produced at the Blackfriars and Globe playhouses. The controversy, in which Henry Evans was of course concerned, is referred to in *Hamlet*, Act II., Scene 2. Rosencrantz explains that the tragedians in whom the city were wont to take a delight were forced to seek audiences in the provinces. Their " inhibition " was due to " the late innovation." " An eyrie " [nest] of children, " little eyases " [hawks], were " now the fashion," and they so " assailed the common stages " that many wearing rapiers " were afraid of goose quills " and dared " scarce come thither."

3

*Hamlet.* What ! are they children ?  Who maintains 'em ?
How are they escoted [paid] ?  Will they pursue the quality
[actors' profession] no longer than they can sing ?  Will they
not say afterwards, if they should grow themselves to common
players (as it is most like if their means are not better), their
writers do them wrong, to make them exclaim against their
own succession ?

*Rosencrantz.* Faith, there has been much to do on both sides
and the nation holds it no sin to tarre them to controversy;
there was for a while no money bid for argument unless the
poet and the player went to cuffs in the question.

Queen Elizabeth showed her personal approval
of the children of the Chapel Royal by twice
inviting them to perform in Court in the winters
of 1601 and of 1602, and Sir Dudley Carleton,
the Court gossip, wrote on December 29th, 1601,
that the Queen dined that day privately with Lord
Hunsdon, the Lord Chamberlain.  He adds: " I
came even now from the Blackfriars, where I saw
her at the play with all her *candidæ auditrices.*"
Lord Hunsdon's house was in the precincts of
Blackfriars, and it is pointed out that the performance probably took place at the residence of
the Lord Chamberlain, as the Queen was not in the
habit of attending public theatres.  The boys of
Blackfriars in 1603-04, when James I. had come
to the throne, entered the service of Queen Anne
of Denmark, and were given the new title of " Children of the Queen's Revels."  Having, however,

34

become offensive in their behaviour, and produced some plays which contained political allusions distasteful to the Court, the company was dismissed by Philip Herbert, Earl of Montgomery, as Chamberlain of the Household. Among the subjects touched upon by the plays which gave such sharp offence to the Court was that of the Welsh mines, which in those days, as in these, appear to have provided other inflammatory stuff than coal.

At the Globe Theatre a Shakespeare Company held the boards, the members of which occasionally gave performances in the provinces. Upon several occasions they visited Shrewsbury and once, in 1593, Bristol, and there is a record of Shakespeare having accompanied them upon that occasion. There is no evidence to prove that he ever visited Wales, although there are traditions to that effect in Breconshire and Pembrokeshire. With the Breconshire tradition we shall deal more fully in another chapter. As regards Pembrokeshire, the reader will recollect that it figures in several of the historical plays, Milford Haven being the chief landing-place for expeditions from France, Italy, and Ireland. One of the four chief Roman roads was Ryknield Street, which name was sometimes given to the whole route from the extremity of South Wales to the Tyne. Shakespeare has made repeated allusions to it in *Cymbeline*, in which Milford Haven, on the western extension of the Ryknield Street, is mentioned as the port from which the voyage to Italy was made, and as the landing-place for the " legions garrison'd in Gallia " (*Cymbeline*, IV. 2). Remembering that Shakespeare, like all poets, instinctively made use of his actual experiences, we may regard these constant references to Milford as tending to support the tradition which speaks of him as visiting Wales, but it is improbable that we shall ever know the truth. Although he may well have known the nearer parts of Wales, it is hardly likely that he would have gone as far afield as Milford. It is far more probable that his Welsh fellow-townsmen had spoken to him of Milford Haven as the great port of South Wales, and the starting-point of long and adventurous voyages.

# CHAPTER III

SHAKESPEARE was born in the sixth year of the reign of Queen Elizabeth, and the Spanish Armada had been defeated about two years after he had left Stratford-on-Avon for London. Elizabeth died in 1603, so that Shakespeare outlived her by thirteen years, during which time he was a subject of James I., the only child of Mary Queen of Scots and Henry Darnley, grandson of Margaret Tudor. Mary Queen of Scots was herself a grandchild of Margaret Tudor by her first husband, James IV., Darnley being the grandchild of Margaret Tudor by her second husband, the Earl of Angus.

Elizabeth's was the concluding reign of a dynasty founded indirectly by Owen Tudor, a Welsh gentleman of a noble Anglesea family. The Tudors traced their descent from Cadwaladr Fendigaid, the last British King, who died, according to *Brut y Tywysogion*, or the Chronicle of the Princes, in A.D. 681, after a reign of twelve years. The royal blood both of North and of South Wales ran in their veins. They fought for Llywelyn the

37

Great; they were represented at Creçy and Agincourt; they supported their kinsman Glendower; and they had married into the French and English Royal Families. " It was," writes Sir Owen M. Edwards, " partly good fortune and partly their own determination that their fortune should be good that brought them to the brilliant position they occupied during the sixteenth century, and enabled them to become the creators of modern Britain in all the essential aspects of its history."

Queen Elizabeth was the only child of Henry VIII. and Anne Boleyn, who was his second wife. Anne Boleyn was the daughter of Sir Thomas Boleyn and his wife, Lady Elizabeth, daughter of the Duke of Norfolk. The King was disappointed that she did not bring him a male heir, and she was beheaded on May 19th, 1536, on Tower Green. " From childhood," says Dixon, " she had been a bright and elfin creature, one in whom the Saxon depths were lighted up with Celtic fire." There is a tradition that the unfortunate Queen lived for a time at Tymawr, near Porthcawl. It is also said that the Williamses of Penpont, in Brecon, once bore the name of Bullen, or Boleyn, and that Anne was an offshoot of this ancient stock.

Elizabeth ascended the throne at a time when the fortunes of England were at a very low ebb,

38

but she made her reign one of the most glorious periods of English history. She was a popular monarch, in spite of her impetuous will, her harshness and pride, and her furious outbursts of temper, which historians attribute to her Tudor blood.

The Elizabethan period, in addition to being a time of great progress and prosperity, was also a time of ceaseless conflict. " The human mind, awakening from the sleep of Feudalism and the Dark Ages, fastened on all the problems that are inherent to human society, problems which even at the present day are not half solved. The clash of opinions went on in all branches of human knowledge. Men were digging down to the very roots of things—Politics, Science, Philosophy, and Religion " (Arber).

The Spanish menace having been disposed of, the commerce of England advanced by leaps and bounds. Daring sailors, the majority of whom were Devonshire men, sailed the high seas in search of adventure, and opened up new and profitable markets for English commerce. Visions of galleons " loaded to the brim with pearls and diamonds and ingots of silver " stirred the popular imagination, and England was in a state of continual ferment and effervescence. With prosperity came an increase of comfort, luxury, and enjoyment. In-

39

tellectually, also, great progress was made. For the instruction of the youth of the country Grammar Schools were established throughout the provinces, while through the medium of the classical translations sent out from the Universities the people were made familiar with the literary treasures of Greece and Rome.

At Christmastide of 1594 Shakespeare received a summons to act at Court with the most famous actors of the day. It is believed that this was due to the interest which Elizabeth took in his plays. *Love's Labour's Lost* was given at Whitehall at Christmas, 1597. Elizabeth, if we may credit tradition, did not conceal her admiration for Falstaff, and Ben Jonson bears testimony to Shakespeare's popularity with James I., as well as with Elizabeth, in his elegy on Shakespeare, where he speaks of—

> Those flights upon the banks of Thames,
> That so did take Eliza and our James.

Shakespeare probably saw Queen Elizabeth for the first time upon the occasion of her State visit to Kenilworth Castle on July 9th, 1575, ten years after her gift of it to Leicester. He was then eleven years of age. Kenilworth lies within easy distance of Stratford-on-Avon, and Shakespeare would have had no difficulty in joining the im-

40

mense throng which assembled in the neighbourhood of the Castle to extend to the Tudor Queen
a loyal and enthusiastic welcome. We may be
sure that among the onlookers there were large
numbers of Welsh folk from across the border.
The spectacular approach of Elizabeth has been
graphically described by Sir Walter Scott in
*Kenilworth*, and we can easily imagine the powerful
impression which the cavalcade must have made
upon the youthful mind of the Poet.

" Pedantry, novelty, the allegory of Italy, the
chivalry of the Middle Ages, the mythology of
Rome, the English bear-fight, pastorals, superstition, farce, all took their turn " (says Green) " in
the entertainment which Lord Leicester provided
for the Queen at Kenilworth. A ' wild man '
from the Indies chanted her praises, and Echo
answered him. Elizabeth turned from the greet-
ings of sibyls and giants to deliver the enchanted
lady from her tyrant ' Sans Pitie,' shepherdesses
welcomed her with carols of the spring, while
Ceres and Bacchus poured their corn and grapes
at her feet."

Sir Walter Scott believed that the celebrated
vision of Oberon might have been inspired by the
impression which the child Shakespeare received
upon this occasion, and the well-known lines alluding

to the Queen are said to have met with Her Majesty's approval:

> That very time I saw (but thou could'st not),
> Flying between the cold moon and the earth,
> Cupid all arm'd: a certain aim he took
> At a fair vestal throned by the west,
> And loos'd his love shaft smartly from his bow,
> As it should pierce a hundred thousand hearts.
> But I might see young Cupid's fiery shaft
> Quench'd in the chaste beams of the watery moon,
> And the imperial votaress passed on,
> In maiden meditation, fancy free.

The possibility that Shakespeare was a witness of the Kenilworth pageant becomes almost a probability when we learn that a relative of his mother's (Edward Arden) was at that time in Leicester's service.

How deeply Shakespeare was impressed by the talents, the wisdom, and the instinct for statesmanship of the Tudor sovereign—or how neatly he was able to flatter a vain King on demand—is revealed by the following noble prophecy which he puts into the mouth of Cranmer in the christening scene at the end of the play of *King Henry VIII.:*

> *Cranmer.*                    Let me speak, sir,
> For heaven now bids me; and the words I utter
> Let none think flattery, for they'll find 'em truth.
> This royal infant—heaven still move about her !—
> Though in her cradle, yet now promises
> Upon this land a thousand thousand blessings,
> Which time shall bring to ripeness: she shall be—

But few now living can behold that goodness—
A pattern to all princes living with her,
And all that shall succeed: Saba* was never
More covetous of wisdom and fair virtue
Than this pure soul shall be. . . .
                        Her own shall bless her;
Her foes shake like a field of beaten corn,
And hang their heads with sorrow: good grows with her:
In her days every man shall eat in safety,
Under his own vine, what he plants; and sing
The merry songs of peace to all his neighbours. . . .
Nor shall this peace sleep with her: but as when
The bird of wonder dies, the maiden phœnix,
Her ashes new create another heir,
As great in admiration as herself;
So shall she leave her blessedness to one,
When heaven shall call her from this cloud of darkness,
Who from the sacred ashes of her honour
Shall star-like rise, as great in fame as she was,
And so stand fix'd: peace, plenty, love, truth, terror,
That were the servants to this chosen infant,
Shall then be his, and like a vine grow to him:
Wherever the bright sun of heaven shall shine,
His honour and the greatness of his name
Shall be, and make new nations: he shall flourish,
And, like a mountain cedar, reach his branches
To all the plains about him: our children's children
Shall see this, and bless heaven.
   *King.*                        Thou speakest wonders,
   *Cran.* She shall be, to the happiness of England,
An aged princess; many days shall see her,
And yet no day without a deed to crown it.
Would I had known no more! but she must die,
She must, the saints must have her; yet a virgin,
A most unspotted lily shall she pass
To the ground, and all the world shall mourn her.

* The Queen of Sheba.

43

It will be noted that reference is here made to the early settlements on the shores of New England.

We catch a glimpse of the Tudor Queen through the Welsh eyes of Lord Herbert of Cherbury in that most individual of books, his *Autobiography*, wherein he says: " Curiosity, rather than ambition, brought me to Court (in 1600); and as it was the manner of those times for all men to kneel down before the great Queen Elizabeth, who then reigned, I was likewise upon my knees in the presence-chamber when she passed by to the chapel at Whitehall. As soon as she saw me she stopped, and swearing her usual oath [' God's Death '], demanded, ' Who is this ?' Everybody there present looked upon me, but no man knew me, until Sir James Croft, a pensioner, finding the Queen stayed, returned back and told who I was, and that I had married Sir William Herbert of St. Julian's daughter. The Queen hereupon looked attentively upon me, and swearing again her ordinary oath, said, ' It is a pity he was married so young,' and thereupon gave her hand to kiss twice, both times gently clapping me on the cheek."

# CHAPTER IV

## SOME NOTABLE WELSHMEN OF SHAKESPEARE'S TIME

THERE were many notable Welshmen of the latter part of the sixteenth century whom Shakespeare may have known personally, or of whose careers, at all events, he must have been an interested spectator. Other eminent men were of Welsh extraction, or connected with great Welsh families. Among these, it appears, was no less a person than William Cecil, Lord Burghley. According to Hume (*The Great Lord Burghley*), Cecil, who throughout his life was a diligent student of heraldry and genealogy, devoted considerable attention to the subject of his remote ancestry, and Camden was at pains to trace his descent to a Robert Sitsilt, a gentleman of Wales in the time of William Rufus (1091). There is a written pedigree at Hatfield House, annotated and continued by William Cecil, which traces the descent of the statesman's grandfather, Richard Sitsilt, who died in 1508, possessing considerable estates in Monmouthshire and Herefordshire, to the ancient Welsh family of Sitsilt. In his *Tudor Statesmen*

45

Innes tells us that David, one of the sons of Richard Sitsilt, elected to modify his name into Cecil on migrating to Lincolnshire, where he prospered greatly. Jeyes, in his *Life and Times of the Marquis of Salisbury, K.G.*, says that in the latter part of the fifteenth century one of the members of the Cecil family, whose name was David Cyssell, acted as Sheriff of Northamptonshire and Alderman of Stamford.

Another of Elizabeth's trusted counsellors was William Herbert, the first Earl of Pembroke (second creation), of whom Sir Owen M. Edwards writes: " He could neither read nor write, though he signs his name in capital letters. It is said of him also that he only knew his own language well. It is to be supposed that the language was Welsh. . . . But the big, bony, red-haired Welshman with the sharp eye and stern look won the regard of Henry VIII., Edward VI., Mary, and Elizabeth, successively, and he served them all faithfully and well. When so many men who could read and write lost their heads, Herbert rivalled Cecil as an adroit politician. He helped Henry VIII. to suppress the monasteries; he relieved Exeter with two thousand Welshmen during the Cornish rising against Somerset; he helped Northumberland to secure the succession of Lady Jane Grey; he carried the Sword of State before Mary on her wedding day; he persuaded Elizabeth to take up a Protestant policy. He was the chief figure in all the sudden changes which brought so many men low, and died in peace."

The Herbert family came of a redoubtable Welsh stock. Dircks tells us of a Herbert (*Herbertus Camararius*) who came over as a comrade of the Conqueror. Early in the thirteenth century a descendant of his had lordships granted him in Wales; his grandson, Peter Fitz Reginald, married a Welsh heiress, and for several generations his successors followed his example, with the result that the position of the family was consolidated in the south of Wales

Sir William Herbert, eighth in descent from Reginald Herbert, had a son of his own name, who became celebrated in the civil wars for his services to the House of York. He received from Edward IV. large grants of land in Wales and elsewhere. He was summoned to Parliament as Baron Herbert of Chepstow, and in 1461 was created Earl of Pembroke. In 1469 he marched northwards at the head of 18,000 Welshmen to suppress a dangerous Lancastrian rising in the North of England. He was defeated at the Battle of Danes Moor, near Edgecote. Taken to Northampton as a prisoner, he was later beheaded. His son and successor surrendered the title of Earl of Pembroke to Edward IV., and was instead created Earl of Huntingdon. He died leaving only a daughter, who carried the Barony of Herbert of Chepstow into the family of Somerset (Duke of Beaufort). The William Herbert who played so important a part in Court and on battle-field in the reigns of the last four Tudor monarchs was the son of Sir Richard Herbert, Kt., of Ewyas, by Margaret, daughter and heiress of St. Matthew Cradock, Kt., of Swansea. He married Anne, daughter of Thomas, Lord Parr, sister of Catherine Parr, the last wife of Henry VIII., and in 1551 was created Baron Herbert of Cardiff and Earl of Pembroke. He obtained from the same King and Edward VI. the lordship of Glamorgan. He was Captain-General of the English army in France in 1557. It is recorded that "he rode on February 7th, 1552-53, to his mansion of Bayard Castle with 300 horse to his retinue, of which 100 were gentlemen in plain blue cloth with chains of gold and badges of a dragon on their sleeves." The family crest is a dragon. His son held, among other offices, that of President of the Council of Wales. The second Earl's third wife was the daughter of Sir Henry Sidney, K.G. She it was

48

who was the mother of William, the third Earl, who, as already intimated, has been identified with the " W. H." of Shakespeare's *Sonnets*— whether rightly so we shall consider in another chapter.

Owing to the outbreak of the plague towards the end of 1603, the Court of James I. was temporarily transferred to Wilton, the residence of William Herbert. Late in November, Shakespeare's Company of King's Players went thither in answer to a royal summons, and a performance was given before the new King. Seven years after Shakespeare's death his admirers and fellow-actors collected and published his plays, the collection being known as the First Folio. William Herbert was then Lord Chamberlain. The dedication of the Folio ran as follows: " To the most noble and incomparable paire of brethren William, Earl of Pembroke, etc., Lord Chamberlaine to the King's most excellent majesty, and Philip, Earl of Montgomery, etc., Gentleman to His Majesties Bedchamber. Both knights of the Noble Order of the Garter and our singular good Lords." One portion of the dedication alludes to past favours in these words: " But since your lordships have beene pleas'd to thinke these trifles something, heretofore; and have prosequuted both them and their

4 49

Author living with so much favour: we hope that (they outliving him and he not having the fate common with some to be exequutor to his owne writings) you will use the like indulgence toward them you have done unto their parent. There is a great difference whether any Booke choose his Patrones or find them: this hath done both. For so many were your lordships' likings of the severall parts when they were acted as before they were published, the Volume asked to be yours."

Lord Herbert of Cherbury followed the ancestral policy with reference to marriage, espousing Mary, his cousin, the daughter and heiress of Sir. William Herbert of St. Julian's, between Caerleon and Newport. He was born at Eyeton-on-Severn, Shropshire, in 1583, and died in 1648. He went campaigning in the Low Counties in 1610 and 1614, and was appointed Ambassador at Paris in 1619. He is regarded as one of the forerunners of the deistical movement of the eighteenth century. Philosopher, historian, diplomatist, courtier, dandy, lover, swashbuckler, mystic, he was a typical child of his age and a typical Welshman. His *Autobiography*, eminently readable, intensely human, and racy of the man, should be familiar to every student of Welsh character.

George Herbert, the younger brother of Lord

Herbert of Cherbury, was born at Montgomery Castle in 1593, and died in 1633. In 1618 he was appointed reader of rhetoric at Cambridge, and in 1619 public orator. In 1626 he was given the Lincoln prebend of Leighton Bromswold, Hunts, and in 1630 received the living of Bemerton, near Salisbury. Here he devoted his leisure to the writing of devotional poetry, his *Temple* being even better known than his brother's *Autobiography*.

It was announced during the Shakespearian revival in 1741 that *The Merchant of Venice* and the *Winter's Tale* had not been performed for a century, and that *All's Well that End's Well* had been last acted in Shakespeare's lifetime. It is clear, however, from some notes of playgoing kept by Simon Forman, a London quack doctor and astrologer, that the *Winter's Tale* was performed at the Globe on May 15th, 1611. We also learn something about its first appearance from the old Office Book kept by Sir Henry Herbert, Master of the Revels to Charles I. " Nothing had been heard of it for nearly a century," writes Mr. Elton, " when it was found by a curious accident. Horace Walpole was editing the *Life of Lord Herbert of Cherbury* from a stained and torn MS. at Lymore, and had made vain inquiries about a duplicate

once belonging to Lord Herbert's brother, Sir
Henry Herbert of Ribbisford. At last, in the year
1727, this duplicate was sent to Lord Powis by a
gentleman who had bought the estate at Ribbisford; it appeared that a great oak chest had been
allowed to go with the house, and in this chest
were found the duplicate ' Life ' and various books
and papers, including the Office Book of Sir Henry
Herbert, with notes from August, 1623, onwards.
On the 19th of August, 1623, Sir Henry made
a note of a visit from old Mr. Heminge: ' For the
King's players. An olde playe called *Winter's
Tale*, formerly allowed of by Sir George Bucke
and likewise by mee on Mr. Hemmings his worde
that there was nothing profane added or reformed
thogh the allowed booke was missing; and therefore
I returned it without a fee.' ''

A famous Welsh antiquary of Elizabeth's reign
was Sir John Price, one of the descendants of
Einon Sais. He was born at Oxford, and admitted
Bachelor of Civil Law in 1534. He studied at
the Inns of Court, and after being called to the Bar
was, it is said, noticed by King Henry VIII., by
whom he was appointed one of the Council of the
Court of the Marches. He married Joan, daughter
of John Williams of Southwark. John Williams
was a son of William Evan, or William Morgan,

of Whitchurch, and elder brother of Morgan Williams, who married a daughter of Walter Cromwell of Putney, from whom descended Oliver Cromwell, the Protector. Sir John Price took a very active part in the Union of Wales with England, and was supposed to be the person who dictated the petition to Henry VIII. He was knighted by Henry, and died probably in 1572.

After the dissolution of the monasteries in the reign of Henry VIII., the Priory Lands, Brecon, were granted to Sir John Price, and from him descended, through the female line, to the present owner, the Earl of Camden. In his *History of Brecknockshire*, Theophilus Jones, the Welsh historian, says: " To his son Richard Price, who was well known and received at the Court of London during the reigns of Edward VI., Philip and Mary, and the beginning of Elizabeth's, I have reason to believe that Shakespeare was indebted for ' that remnant of Welsh flannel ' *Sir Hugh Evans*, a character (if such it may be called) which seems to be introduced merely to amuse the audience with the jargon and phraseology of the Briton, and to make fritters of the English tongue, in which, as in everything else the poet has undertaken, he has most admirably succeeded. Sir Hugh Evans [the Breconshire clergyman] was the protégé of

53

our antiquary, Sir John Price, and his son Richard, the latter of whom presented him with the living of Merthyr Cynog in Breconshire in 1572." We are not, I think, to read Jones as suggesting that the real Sir Hugh Evans, whom Shakespeare may never have met, was necessarily the prototype of the Windsor parson; but rather that the dramatist may have been indebted to Price for his name, and perhaps for anecdotes relating to the actual Evans; in short, that Shakespeare may have reproduced the personal peculiarities or the accent of Price, and borrowed the name of his protégé, the country clergyman, perhaps to blend them with the characteristics of his old friend Thomas Jenkins.

Shakespeare's acquaintance with another prominent Welshman seems to have been established with something approaching certainty by Sir Sidney Lee. "Sir John Salisbury, a Welsh country gentleman of Lleweni, Denbighshire, and by two years Shakespeare's junior," he writes, "married in early life Ursula Stanley, the natural daughter of the fourth Earl of Derby, who was at one time patron of Shakespeare's theatrical company. Sir John's surname is usually spelt Salusbury. Dr. Johnson's friend, Mrs. Thrale (afterwards Mrs. Piozzi), whose maiden name was Salusbury, was a

54

direct descendant. Sir John Salisbury spent much of his time in London, being knighted in 1601. A man of literary culture, he could turn a stanza with some deftness, and was a generous patron of many Welsh and English bards, who wrote much in honour of himself and his family. . . . Robert Chester was evidently a confidential protégé, closely associated with the knight's Welsh home. It is clear that Sir John was acquainted with Ben Jonson and other men of letters in the capital, and that Shakespeare and the rest good-naturedly contributed to Chester's volume by way of showing regard for a minor Mæcenas of the day." The volume referred to is Chester's *Love's Martyr ; or, Rosalin's Complaint, shadowing the Truth of Love in the Constant Fate of the Phœnix and the Turtle,* to which Shakespeare contributed the poem reprinted at the end of the modern editions of his works.

Shakespeare may also have come into contact with John Williams, goldsmith to James I., whom Drayton (in his introduction to the seven long poems which he devoted to Wales) describes as that " true lover of his countrie (as of all ancient and noble things) Mr. John Williams his majesty's goldsmith, my dear and worthy friend."

The formation of the New River to carry the

55

springs of the River Lea to the heart of the City of London, in the year 1613, was largely due to a distinguished Welshman, Sir Hugh Myddelton, whose persistence overcame unending difficulties and opposition, and the first official act of his brother, Sir Thomas Myddelton, who was elected Lord Mayor of London the same year, was to perform the opening ceremony. Sir Hugh Myddelton was born at Galch Hill, Denbigh, about the year 1560. There is a tradition that he and Sir Walter Raleigh used to sit together at the door of the former's shop and smoke the newly introduced weed tobacco, greatly to the amazement of the passers-by. He likewise entered into the new trade of clothmaking with great energy, and followed it with so much success that, in a speech delivered by him in the House of Commons between 1614 and 1617 on the proposed cloth patent, he was able to state that he and his partner employed several hundred families.

Sir Thomas Myddelton, who was born in 1550, purchased in 1595 Chirk Castle, an Edwardian stronghold in his native county erected by Roger de Mortimer in the reign of Edward I, He entered Parliament in 1597–98 as Member for Merionethshire. Another member of this family, Captain William Myddelton, born in

1556, finished his translation of the Psalms on January 24th, 1595–96, at Scutum, in the West Indies, but the work, which was edited for the press by another Denbighshire man, Thomas Salesbury of Clocaenog, was not published until 1603. He was buried at Antwerp.

An anonymous writer signing himself " E. R. W." gives in the *Welsh Outlook* for March, 1915, the following among other particulars of the life of Sir Roger Williams, who is suggested as a probable prototype of Shakespeare's Fluellen (see Chapter XII.): He was born at Penrhos in Monmouthshire. He probably spent some time at Brasenose College, Oxford, and became a page in the Earl of Pembroke's employ. He saw service first in the storming of St. Quentin in 1557. The rest of his life he spent as a soldier of fortune, winning for himself a European repute for reckless and personal daring. It is little wonder (adds the writer) that pamphlets of his achievements in the wars entitled *Newes from Sir Roger Williams* sold like hot cakes in the streets of London, and in Chapman's play, *Byron's Conspiracy*, Henry of Navarre, no doubt for the benefit of the " groundlings," is made to refer to the " swelling ardour " of Colonel Williams. With the Queen he was on indifferent terms : the soldierly bluntness of his speech and the persistency with

which he advocated more radical measures against
Spain (thus compromising her policy of "wise
passiveness") did not tend to conciliate her.
"I would refuse no hazard in the Queen's service,"
he wrote in 1584, "but I do persuade myself she
makes no account of me"; and he feared he would
have to serve Duke Mathias in Hungary, or one
of the Turkish pashas against Persia. On one of
his appearances at Court to prefer some suit,
Elizabeth, observing a new pair of boots on his
legs, claps her hand to her nose, and cries, "Fah,
Williams! prithee begone; thy boots stink!" "Tut,
tut, madame!" he replied, with rough wit; "'tis
my suit that stinks." In July, 1595, when visiting
England, he had the satisfaction of being received
at Greenwich by Her Majesty and all the Court
in "a friendly public welcome." He died in
December, 1595, and was buried in St. Paul's Cathedral "in a very good martiall sort," and among the
mourners were "all the warlike men of the City of
London." He was "literatured" in the wars like
Captain Gower, as witness his "Brief Discourse
of War, with his opinions concerning some part of
martiall discipline," nor could Fluellen (suggests
the writer), in his heated disputes with Captain
Macmorris, have outdone the vigour with which Sir
Roger entered into controversy with his many critics.

58

We have seen that Shakespeare would have had many opportunities of studying the Welsh character in his boyhood and early youth among his schoolfellows and fellow-townsmen, and in the person of the schoolmaster, Thomas Jenkins. Subsequent opportunities occurred during his association with Welshmen in London and at the Court.

That much interest was taken by Englishmen in things Welsh at this period is evident from the numerous references to Wales and Welshmen to be found in the works of the playwrights of the sixteenth and early seventeenth century. In many cases Welsh phrases and even sentences are introduced, as, for example: " I do love *cawse boby*, good rosted cheese " (Andrew Borde's *Book of Knowledge*, 1542), and " *Nos da diu cata why* " (Nashe, *Gros III.*, 1596). In 1619 King James (Elizabeth's successor) witnessed the performance of an anti-masque written by Ben Jonson " for the sake of variety and the King's amusement," entitled *For the Honour of Wales*, in which the characters are Griffith, Jenkin, and Evan, a Welsh attorney. The work is interlarded with such Welsh expressions as " *Gad vyn lonyth* " (Let me alone); " *Velhy* " (Heyday; or so); " *Tawson* " (Hold your tongue); " *Ble mae yr Brenin ?*" (Where

59

is the King ?); " *Docko Ve* " (There he is); and
" *Strewch* " (Hold your peace). Harpists and
women in Welsh costumes are introduced, and at
the close Griffith talks of the manifold virtues of
the Welsh people.

We know that Ben Jonson once studied a Welsh
Grammar, perhaps as a preparatory measure to
writing the above-mentioned masque.

James Howell,* who has been described as the
prince of letter writers of his age, kept up an
intimate correspondence with Ben Jonson, of whom
he was a loving " son and servitor " In one of
his letters he tells his (literary) " Father, Mr. Ben
Johnson," that he had been unable to " light
upon *Dr. Davies's Welsh* Grammar," but " before
Christmas " he was promised one. When the book
arrived Howell thought it better than any of the
" Accidences " used for teaching Irish and Basque,
but, adds Mr. Elton, " he makes no mention of
the famous Grammar published by Griffith Roberts
at Milan in 1567." In forwarding the volume
Howell writes : " *Father Ben*, you desir'd me lately
to procure you *Dr. Davies's Welsh Grammar*, to
add to those many you have; I have lighted upon

* He was born in 1594, and graduated B.A. at Jesus College,
Oxford. Many interesting extracts from his letters are given
in *William Shakespeare, his Family and Friends*, by C. I. Elton,
K.C. (1904).

one at last, and I am glad I have it in so seasonable a time that it may serve for a New Year's gift, in which quality I send it you. . . ."

> 'Twas a tough task, believe it, thus to tame
> A wild and wealthy Language, and to frame
> Grammatic toils to curb her, so that she
> Now speaks in Rules and sings in Prosody.
> Such is the strength of Art rough things to shape
> And of rude Commons rich Inclosures make.

It is interesting to know that, when Howell was a young man, he was sent to Venice to learn the secrets of glass-making. A monopoly for making glass with pit coal at Swansea had been obtained by William Herbert, Earl of Pembroke, Sir Robert Mansell, and others. The object in using coal, Howell informs us, was " to save those huge Proportions of Wood which were consumed formerly in the glass Furnaces. And this Business, being of that nature that the Workmen are to be had from *Italy*, and the chief Materials from *Spain*, *France*, and other foreign countries, there is need of an agent abroad for this Use."

One of Shakespeare's " fellows "—or members of his own company, who, according to the First Folio, took part in the representation of his dramas —was Nathaniel Field, the son of a Puritanical clergyman, and a native of London. The father died in March, 1587–88. " Nat " Field was one of the Boys of the Chapel Royal, and, like most boy actors, affected female parts. His brother was Theophilus Field, Bishop of Llandaff (1619) and of St. David's (1627). Another of Shakespeare's " fellows," Robert Armin, originally a " prentice " to a goldsmith in Lombard Street, is believed to have been the author of the drama *The Valiant Welshman*, by R. A., Gent. (1615).

Another notable contemporary of Shakespeare's, whom he may have met through Jonson, was Inigo Jones, the reviver of classical architecture in England. He was of Welsh descent, and his arms are said to have been those of a Denbighshire family of the name. Born in London on July 15th, 1573, he was at first an apprentice to a joiner; but his talents having attracted the notice of William Herbert, the third Earl of Pembroke (second creation), the latter supplied him with the means of visiting Italy for the purpose of studying landscape painting. He went to Venice, where the works of Palladio inspired him with a taste for architecture, and he afterwards devoted all his energies to the pursuit of that branch of art. In 1620, he was appointed one of the commissioners for repairing St. Paul's Cathedral, but this work was not commenced until 1623. He was much employed in preparing masques for the entertainment of the Court and in building the banquetting hall at Whitehall. He designed the scenery for Ben Jonson's *Masque of Blackness*, given at Whitehall, but at a later date Jonson held him up to ridicule in *Bartholomew Fair*. In the church of St. Mary at Llanrwst, North Wales, which was built in the fifteenth century, is a chapel erected in 1633 by Sir Richard Wynne of Gwydir from the design of Inigo Jones. The bridge at Llanrwst, was also built by Jones. In 1648 the south side of Wilton House was destroyed by fire, and was rebuilt by Philip Herbert, fourth Earl of Pembroke, with the advice of Inigo Jones, and there is a belief that Jones designed the old Stepney mansion at Llanelly. As an author, Jones is known by a work relating to Stonehenge, which he pronounced to be a Roman temple dedicated to Cœlus, an opinion which has long been superseded. He realised a handsome fortune, but being a Roman Catholic and a partisan of royalty, he suffered severely during the Civil War, and died, worn out by sorrow and adversity, on July 5th, 1651.

## CHAPTER V

### SHAKESPEARE'S ATTITUDE TOWARD THE WELSH

In 1896, as the first Chancellor of the University of Wales, King Edward VII., then Prince of Wales, delivered an address which, affording, as it does, an excellent idea of the intellectual status of the Welsh in the Tudor period, and containing an interesting reference to the Welsh characters of Shakespeare, may usefully be quoted at some length:

"From very early times, in spite of difficulties and adverse circumstances, the Welsh people have seldom failed to display a marked love for literature and learning. Even in so remote an age as the sixth century, works were produced in which scholars perceive a standard of literary taste very noteworthy for those early days. Schools of systematic learning in Wales existed only in its monasteries, and from St. David's came forth Asser to aid Alfred the Great in his work amongst his West Saxon subjects. Throughout the Middle Ages we find the profession of letters held in universal respect in Wales, its exponents protected by privileges and treated everywhere as honoured guests and the objects of popular regard; while Welsh scholars absent from home constituted a conspicuous element in the cosmopolitan crowds which flocked to mediæval Oxford. The troubles of the fourteenth and fifteenth centuries fatally obstructed the development of permanent educational institutions west of Offa's Dyke; but when England under the Tudors opened its colleges to the scholastic ambition of Wales, Welsh students were again found thronging to the English Universities, and adding distinguished names to the rolls of the learned professions. Nor is it without significance that *Shakespeare, with his intuitive perception of character, representing at this epoch three highly finished portraits of Welshmen, depicted them all— the soldier, the divine, and the feudal chieftain—as men of thought and learning."*

Shakespeare indeed did this, but he did more: he embodied in his three Welsh personages the outstanding characteristics of the Welsh race. In the character of Glendower we are presented with the mystical, idealistic, and the poetical side of the Celtic nature; Sir Hugh Evans is the shrewd, homely, Bible-loving Welshman; while Fluellen displays the war-like, chivalrous, and loyal attributes of the Welsh people. It will thus be seen

5

that in his representation of the Welsh character Shakespeare rose above the racial prejudices of his fellow-countrymen, which found congenial expression in the old Anglo-Saxon doggerel wherein Taffy is described as a persistent purloiner of other people's goods. Indeed, we may claim Shakespeare as a champion of Welsh nationality, for in *King Henry V.* the fiery Fluellen makes an English braggart eat the leek, while Gower severely admonishes Pistol for ridiculing the Welsh.

There is one trait, however, in the character of the Welsh people which Shakespeare has not represented—namely, their mirthfulness, although we catch a glimpse of it in the gusto with which Sir Hugh Evans " turns the tables " on " Mine Host of the Garter," and urges his fairies to " pinse and burn " the too fleshly Falstaff.

Many explanations may be advanced to account for Shakespeare's friendly interest in and sympathetic attitude towards the Welsh people. To begin with, he lived at a time when a Queen of Welsh descent occupied the throne of England—a Queen to whom he was personally known, and who, tradition tells us, was proud of her Welsh lineage. A second reason that suggests itself is that through his association with Thomas Jenkins and other Stratford citizens Shakespeare may have come

66

to cherish a liking for the people from beyond the marches. It is also probable that he was influenced by his friend Drayton, the Warwickshire poet, who had a considerable knowledge of Wales, and wrote much that was highly complimentary to the Principality. A fourth, and it seems to us a very plausible, explanation of Shakespeare's interest in the Welsh nation may be found in the circumstance that the poet was evidently convinced of the truth of the tradition that his paternal ancestors fought at Bosworth Field on the side of Richmond, and received from Henry VII., " in reward for valiant and faithful services, tenements and lands in Warwickshire." There was also a claim made that his mother, Mary Arden, was descended of an ancient and distinguished family connected with " John Arden, Esquire, of the Body of Henry VII." The poet's father certainly applied for a grant of arms in the year 1596, and on October 20th of the same year a draft, which is still extant in the College of Arms, was prepared under the direction of William Dethick, Garter King of Arms, granting John Shakespeare's petition. Dethick declared that he had been by credible report informed that the applicant's " parentes and late antecessors were for theire valeant and faithfull service advanced and rewarded by the most prudent Prince

67

King Henry VII. of famous memorie sythence whiche tyme they have continued at those partes [*i.e.*, Warwickshire] in good reputacion and credit." The question as to the accuracy or otherwise of the declaration made to the Garter King of Arms does not concern us here. It is sufficient for our purpose to know that Shakespeare himself believed that his ancestors had fought for and had been rewarded by Henry the Welsh King.

Shakespeare's Welshmen are all good men and true. Henry V. (" Harry of Monmouth ") is " a mirror of all Christian kings "; Henry VII. is " England's hope "; Glendower is brave and affable and generous; Sir Hugh Evans is peaceful and pious; Fluellen is loyal and chivalrous; the Welsh captain is " trusty "; the supporters of Henry VI. in the Principality are loyal and " loving "; Belarius claims that those who come from Cambria are " gentle " and honest; and it must not be overlooked that Shakespeare described Queen Elizabeth as " a pattern to all princes," though this remark may be due to the courtier rather than the love of things Welsh. With the exception of Westmorland's report of the Battle of Brynglas there is not a single reflection on the Welsh character in the plays. And it is significant that Shakespeare displayed this independence of judgment at a time when the old Taffy slander was in full currency, and Beaumont and Fletcher considered the speaking of Welsh a proof of dishonesty. It is probable that Shakespeare's defence of " an ancient tradition, begun upon an honourable respect and worn as a memorable trophy of predeceased valour," was due to the knowledge that he had Welsh blood in his veins. In the next chapter we shall see what justification exists for this view of the matter.

# CHAPTER VI

## THE WELSH ANCESTRY OF SHAKESPEARE

MANY prominent Shakespearian biographers have declared that Shakespeare's ancestry cannot be certainly determined, but Mr. Pym Yeatman, F.R.H.S. (of Lincoln's Inn, formerly of Emmanuel College, Cambridge), in his spirited essay, *The Gentle Shakespeare Vindicated*, claims to have discovered a link connecting the Shakespeare family with the Griffins, or Gryffyns, who were descendants of the old Welsh Kings. The author supports his case with a wealth of genealogical and testamentary detail, and explains that the clue which enabled him to complete the Griffin pedigree was found in Mr. Bickly's *Register of the Guild of Knowle*. " To Mr. Bickly, therefore," says Mr. Yeatman, " the world is indebted for this most remarkable and purely accidental discovery, a discovery which, it is perhaps not too much to say of it, utterly confounds the traducers of our Great Poet."

70

Of the Griffin pedigree Mr. Yeatman writes (Chapter XIV.): "The author was searching at Northampton Probate Registry for material to illustrate the history of the Griffin family of that county, and the first will he came to was that of one Francis Griffin of Braybrook, dated February 26th, 37 Henry VIII., in which he refers to his sister, Alys Shakespeare, and, curiously, this was the only will of the family which emanated from that place; nearly all the Griffin wills are to be found in London Registers. It would not appear from this will that Francis Griffin had any other connection with the county of Warwick, although he refers to his cousins, Sir Edward Griffin (afterwards Queen Mary's Attorney-General), who was closely connected with the county; and he also refers to Edmund Bacon, of a family with whom the Griffins were connected by marriage. In 29 Elizabeth Sir Robert Bacon was guardian for the children of Richard Griffin of Warwick, who probably settled there through the marriage of Sir Edward Griffin with the daughter of Sir John Smyth, one of the Barons of the Exchequer—also a Warwickshire man, and allied by marriage to the great Lord Burleigh. There can be little doubt that Sir Edward Griffin mainly owed his advancement

71

to that great man, Sir Nicholas Bacon, who held
the Great Seal at this period, and under whom
he held his office; and therefore there must have
been a close connection between the Griffins, and
their connections, the Shakespeares, even with
Francis Bacon (Lord Verulam), his son, as well
as with the Cecils. In all probability this connection, if worked out, will lead to the discovery
that Alys Griffin (grandmother of the poet) was
akin to the great Lord Bacon."

The pedigree (which Mr. Yeatman publishes)
commences with Griffith, King of South Wales,
son of " Rise ap Tudor, King of South Wales, heir
of King Kadwalider, who died tempe William
Rufus, King of England, and Gwenlian, his wife,
daughter of Griffith ap Kymme, King of North
Wales," and is continued to Edward Griffin of
Berkswell, 1500.

How Alys Griffin entered the Shakespeare family
is shown by the following extract from Mr. Yeatman's chart:

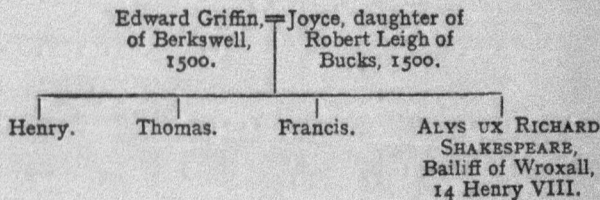

Shakespeare's immediate descent is set forth as follows:

Richard Shakespeare, = Alys, daughter of Edward
Bailiff of Wroxall, had land | Griffin, of Braybrook
at Haseley and Snytter- | and Berkswell. She was
field. *D.* at Snytterfield, | living 1574 (?).
1560-61.

John Shakespeare, = Mary, daughter and    Henry.    Thomas.
of Snytterfield, 1560, | coheir of Robert
and of Stratford-on- | Arden, of Wilme-
Avon, *d.* 1601. | cote, *d.* 1608.

WILLIAM SHAKESPEARE
THE POET.

The interest of this pedigree is obvious. The Celtic strain in Shakespeare's blood may be held to account for the sporadic appearance of genius in an unremarkable middle-class family, as it no doubt accounted for John Shakespeare's restless versatility and almost morbid sensitiveness under adversity. How far Alys Shakespeare was a Welshwoman in her mental habit we cannot know; but we do know that tradition dies hard with the Welsh, and would be more particularly likely to survive in a family proud of its Welsh lineage. Are we justified in picturing the boy Shakespeare as absorbing the folk and fairy lore of the Welsh at the knee of his Welsh grandmother? That is another thing that we can never know. But we do know that he was to some extent familiar with

73

the fairy lore of the Welsh, and interested in Celtic legend; indeed, there are not wanting in the plays little loving touches, as of one referring to cherished memories, which might lead us to believe that his knowledge was acquired in childhood, and that the glamour of childhood lay upon his recollections of Welsh lore and legend. The evidence is almost too tenuous to pursue, yet on reading the plays with the knowledge of the poet's Welsh descent we do actually seem to catch glimpses here and there of Alys Shakespeare telling her little grandson the tales that she herself had heard perhaps from an old Welsh nurse, or perhaps from her own Welsh grandmother.

# CHAPTER VII

## WELSH LEGENDS AND ALLUSIONS IN THE PLAYS

DID Shakespeare, remembering the Welsh legends from his childhood, weave them instinctively into his work, referring to the printed book only to refresh his memory ? Or did he light upon them simply as an omnivorous reader for ever seeking possible ore for refining ? Or was he sent to the written record by chance allusions of his Welsh acquaintances ? However this may be, whether we are to regard him as an industrious miner among the legends of all times and countries, who would sometimes make use of a Welsh legend or fragment of folklore as at other times he discovered material for his plots in translations from the Greek, Latin, or Italian, we find that Welsh literature provided the plots of two of his greatest plays—of *Lear*, perhaps his greatest tragedy, and of *Cymbeline*, which, with all its gracious faults, contains passages unapproachable in their lyrical beauty. Concerning the plot of *Lear*, Gollancz informs us that, " according to some Celtic folklorists, ' Lir ' represents Neptune, his two cruel daughters the rough winds, and Cordelia the gentle zephyr "; and he adds, " I know no better commentary on the tempestuous character of the play. Shakespeare has unconsciously divined the germ of the myth," which, we have no doubt, would greatly surprise Shakespeare.

The story of *Lear* is certainly of extreme antiquity. The oldest extant version is to be found in the *Historia Regum Britanniæ* (" Histories of the Kings of Briton ") of the old Welsh monk Geoffrey of Monmouth,* who was the father of Arthurian romance.

" When Bladud was thus given over to the destines," writes Geoffrey, " his son Lear was next raised to the kingdom, and ruled the country after manly fashion for three score years. He it was that builded the city on the River Soar, that in the British is called Kaerleir, but in Saxon Leicester. Male issue was denied unto him, his only children being three daughters named Goneril, Regan, and Cordelia, whom all he did love with marvellous affection, but most of all the youngest born, to wit Cordelia. And when he began to be upon the verge of eld he thought to divide his kingdom

* He was born about or before A.D. 1100 ; was probably educated by the Benedictines at Monmouth; was appointed Archdeacon of Llandaff about 1140; and in 1152 was consecrated Bishop of the see of St. Asaph, which, however, he never visited. He died in A.D. 1155.

amongst them, and to marry them unto such husbands as were worthy to have them, along with their share of the kingdom. But that he might know which of them was most worthy of the largest share he went unto them to make enquiry of each as to which of them did most love himself."

Geoffrey goes on to tell of the outcome of the test, and describes Lear as " waxing mightily indignant " at the answer of Cordelia. The leading expositors are agreed that Shakespeare used the narrative of Holinshed* (who in turn got it from Geoffrey of Monmouth), but Holinshed, in his version, does not bring out into bold relief, as Geoffrey does, the old man's indignation at the unflattering reply of his youngest daughter. " The father being nothing content with this answer," says Holinshed, " married his two eldest daughters," etc. Shakespeare makes much of the storm of indignation which seized upon the old man at what he considered to be the lack of affection in his youngest daughter, and the thought naturally occurs to us that Shakespeare may have consulted Geoffrey of Monmouth's works as well as

* Holinshed was translator for the press of Reginald Wolfe, who undertook the publication of a *Universal History*. That part of it relating to the British Isles was entrusted chiefly to Holinshed. The first and second editions are dated 1577 and 1587.

77

Holinshed's Chronicles.  In his *Welshman* Thomas Stephens expresses the opinion that Geoffrey's *Histories* had a peculiar fascination for Shakespeare.  This, he says, is shown by many striking passages in his plays.  What those passages are Stephens omits to tell us, but we may find several that will answer this description in *King Lear*, *Cymbeline*, *King Henry IV.*, and *King Henry V.*

One passage in *King Lear* seems to have a bearing upon an episode in the legends of King Arthur and his Knights of the Round Table.  Kent, in the concluding lines of his anathema of Oswald, uses these words:

> Goose, if I had you upon Sarum plain,
> I'd drive ye cackling home to Camelot.

Did Shakespeare consult Malory, whom Leland says was Welsh, as well as Geoffrey and Holinshed?  In this connection it must be remembered that he had many distinguished friends, and could readily have gained access to libraries well provided with the legendary, romantic, and historical literature of all languages and periods. That he did not slavishly follow Holinshed is proved by Sir Sidney Lee, who states that, although the tragedy was mainly founded on Holinshed's Chronicle, Shakespeare grafted on to it the distressing tale of Gloucester and his two sons, which he drew from Sidney's *Arcadia*. Hints of the speeches uttered by Edgar feigning madness were also obtained from Harsnet's *Declaration of Popish Impostures*, and the end which Shakespeare has given to the tragedy differs from Holinshed's. An explanation of the allusion to Camelot is offered by Staunton to the effect that it refers to a quest undertaken in connection with the marriage of King Arthur and Guinevere, the enemies vanquished during this quest being sent to Camelot to make submission to the King.

A passage in *King Lear* which some have regarded as an interpolation may actually be proof of Shakespeare's familiarity with obscure Welsh sources.

Act III., Scene 2, of *King Lear* contains the following lines:

> *Fool.* This is a brave night ! I'll speak a prophecy
>    ere I go:
> When priests are more in word than matter;
> When brewers mar their malt with water;
> When nobles are their tailors' tutors;
> No heretics burn'd but wenches' suitors;
> When every case in law is right;
> No squire in debt, nor no poor knight;
> When slanders do not live in tongues;
> Nor cutpurses come not in throngs;
> Then shall the realm of Albion
> Come to great confusion:

> Then comes the time who lives to see't
> That going shall be used with feet.
> This prophecy Merlin shall make; for
> I live before his time.

As he certainly did; for, according to Geoffrey of Monmouth's reckoning, King Lear was contemporary with Joash, King of Judah. Fleay remarks that " Merlin's Prophecy " is not in Shakespeare's manner; that it was "a mere gag inserted by the Fool Actor to raise a laugh among the groundlings." Here we think Fleay's scholarship was at fault, for the lines do not bear the least resemblance to theatrical " gagging," while they are quite in the spirit of Merlin. It seems more probable that Shakespeare was having a sly dig at the simplicity of some of the prophecies attributed to the great wizard, many of which are extant, and an axample of which we quote from Wilkins' *Wales Past and Present* :

> Truth shall disappear and error spread.
> Men shall be weak of faith and disputing on alternate days.
> And they shall delight in fine garments.
> Bards shall be empty-handed and priests gay,
> Truth shall vanish and denials be frequent.

Although *Cymbeline* is, no less than *Lear*, a work of imagination, Cymbeline himself is by no means so shadowy a figure as Lear, the doubly blind.

80

Cunobelinus, to call him by the Latinised form of his name, was a King of Britain in the first century of our era. His name survives on many coins. He is believed to have been the son of Cassivelaunus, and the father of Caractacus.

" In *Cymbeline*," Sir Sidney Lee tells us, " Shakespeare freely adapted a fragment of British history taken from Holinshed, interweaving with it a story of Boccaccio's *Decameron* (Day 2, Novel IX.). The plot of the banishment of the Lord Belarius, who, in revenge for his expatriation, kidnapped the King's young sons, and brought them up with him in the recesses of the mountains, is Shakespeare's invention."

These mountains were situated in Wales, and with regard to the name Belarius, Thorndike conjectures that it was suggested to Shakespeare by the Bellario of Beaumont and Fletcher's *Philaster*. Shakespeare's Belarius, while in Wales, adopted the name of Morgan, and Charles Wilkins suggests as a possible derivative " Pelagius," the Latinised name for Morgan. Pelagius was a noteworthy character in the Wales of the fifth century. His real name was Heresiarch Morgan. Morgan, or Pelagius, was a learned and holy man of Bangor Iscoed who won great celebrity by his brilliant talents, but entertaining different religious con-

6

victions from his brethren, he was denounced as a heretic. He made a considerable noise in the world, and Shakespeare may have read of him. The suggestion may seem far-fetched; yet we must remember that Shakespeare's mind was dwelling on Wales while writing this scene, which, we are told, was his own invention. Belarius, with the two royal children, retires to a cave in Pembrokeshire, "which is said to have been fairly identified as Hoyle's Mouth, near Tenby" (Wilkins). Imogen, the sister of the two lads, is escorted by Pisano on her journey to Milford Haven, ostensibly to greet her husband, but in reality to meet the doom which, in a fit of unjustifiable jealousy, he has prescribed for her. She is persuaded to adopt male attire, for greater security in travelling. When she is told by Pisano that her husband is at Milford Haven she becomes feverishly impatient to reach her destination, as we see from the following lines :

> O ! for a horse with wings ! Hear'st thou, Pisano ?
> He is at Milford Haven. Read and tell me
> How far 'tis. . . .
> To this same blessed Milford. And, by the way,
> Tell me how Wales was made so happy
> As to inherit such a Haven.

Pisano has not the heart to carry out his master's harsh instructions, but leaves Imogen to an uncertain fate. A kindly Providence directs her steps to the cave-dwelling of Belarius and her two brothers, where, under the assumed name of Fidele, she receives a genial welcome. Before leaving her Pisano gives her a cordial which is to be used in case of sickness. One day, during the absence of old Belarius and the boys, she drinks the potion, and thereupon falls into a death-like sleep. When the youths return to the cave they believe her dead, and carrying her frail form to a shady nook Arvigarius, the younger of the brothers expresses his grief in these beautifully tender lines:

> With fairest flowers,
> While summer lasts and I live here, Fidele,
> I'll sweeten thy sad grave. Thou shalt not lack
> The flower that's like thy face, pale primrose, nor
> The azured harebell, like thy veins; no, nor
> The leaf of eglantine, whom not to slander,
> Outsweetened not thy breath.

It is interesting to note that this lament was uttered in a country where the decking of the graves of the dead with flowers is one of the most cherished of its national customs; and it is a curious coincidence that Shakespeare's lines should bear a certain resemblance to the poetic tribute paid by Dafydd ap Gwilym, the famous Welsh poet of the fourteenth century, to the memory of his patron Ivor Hael:

83

" O ! while thy season of flowers and thy tender sprays thick of leaves remain I will pluck the roses from the brakes, the flowers from the meads, the vivid trefoils, beauties of the ground, and the gaily smiling bloom of the verdant herbs; humbly will I lay them on the grave of Ivor."

There are three lines in *Cymbeline* which are quoted as showing Shakespeare's accurate historical knowledge. When Cassivelaunus was beaten and deserted he went through a form of submission to Cæsar, who, after two months in Britain, left for Gaul. Cæsar's conquest of the people was only nominal; it was not a real subjugation. Shakespeare, therefore, as Thomas Stephens points out, was justified by the facts when he put into the mouth of the Queen-wife of Cymbeline the words:

> A kind of conquest
> Cæsar made here; but made not here his brag
> Of *came* and *saw* and *overcame*.

The continuation of the passage contains a reference to Ludstown, the early Celtic name of London:

> For joy thereof
> The fam'd Cassibelan, who was once at point
> (O giglot [*i.e.*, wanton] fortune) to master Cæsar's sword,
> Made Lud's town with rejoicing fires bright
> And Britons strut with courage.

" One Silurian god whose altar was found at Lydney, on the Severn,' says Mr. Ernest Rhys,

" seems to be the same as Llûd, the name better known in English as the Lud of King Lud, and Ludgate Hill." Geoffrey's version is that London was founded by Brute, a descendant of the Trojan Æneas, and called New Troy, or Troy-novant, until the time of Lud, who surrounded it with walls and gave it the name of Caer Lud, or Ludstown, (Lud's dun), and the Trojans, according to Geoffrey, who displays all the cheerful irresponsibility of the mediæval romanticist, were the progenitors of all the Welsh! In the *Mabinogion* (translated from the *Red Book of Hergist* by Lady Charlotte Guest) we have the following : " Beli the Great, the son of Manogan, had three sons, and according to the story he had a fourth son called Llevelys. And after the death of Beli the kingdom of the Island of Britain fell into the hands of Lludd, his eldest son, and Lludd ruled prosperously and rebuilt the walls of London, and encompassed it about with numberless towers. And after that he bade the citizens build houses therein, such as no houses in the kingdom could equal. And, moreover, he was a mighty warrior, and generous and liberal in giving meat and drink to all that sought them. And though he had many castles and cities, this one he loved more than any. And he dwelt therein most part of the year,

85

and therefore it was called Caer Ludd, and at last Caer London. And after the stranger race came there it was called London, or Lwndrys." In Spenser's *Faerie Queene* (II. x. 46) occur the lines:

> [Lud] Built that gate of which his name is hight
> By which he lies entombed solemnly.

Belarius (*Cymbeline*, Act. V., Scene 5) says of himself and the two boys, in answer to a question of the King's:

> In Cambria are we born, and gentlemen;
> Further to boast were neither true nor modest,
> Unless I add, we are honest.

The claim of Belarius, as set forth in the first line, may conceivably have been present to the mind of James I. when he uttered the remark attributed to him in Yorke's *Royal Tribes of Wales*. When King James was visiting Chester he was met by a great number of horsemen, who formed a guard of honour. The weather was warm and the roads dusty, and His Majesty was greatly inconvenienced by the crowd pressing round his coach. So he told one of his attendants to disperse them politely. The nobleman thereupon put his head out of the window and said, " It is the King's pleasure that all who are gentlemen should ride forward." Away they all rode as if for life, save one man. " And

so, sir, you are not a gentleman, then," observed
the King. " Oh yes, please your Majesty," was
the reply; " but hur ceffyl, God help hur, is not so
good." " Every man is a gentleman in Wales,"
remarked His Majesty. In his *Microsmographie*
(1628) Earle remarks, " They [the Welsh] are
born with heraldry in their mouths, and each name
is a pedigree." This Welsh pride of lineage was
evidently known to Shakespeare.

The reader will remember how Fluellen prides
himself upon " the derivation of his birth " (*Henry
V.*, Act III., Scene 3). Giraldus, commenting upon
this Welsh characteristic, says: " The Welsh esteem
noble birth and generous descent above all things,
and are therefore more desirous of marrying into
noble than into rich families. Even the common
people preserve their genealogy, and cannot only
readily recount the names of their grandfathers
and great-grandfathers, but even refer back to the
sixth or seventh generation or beyond them in
this manner: Rhys, son of Gruffydd, son of Rhys,
son of Tewder, son of Eineon, son of Owen, son of
Howel, son of Cadell, son of Roderic Mawr, and so
on." " Genealogies," we are told by Owen, " were
preserved as a principle of necessity under the
ancient British Constitution. A man's pedigree
was in reality his title deed by which he claimed his

87

birthright in the country. Everyone was obliged to show his descent through nine generations in order to be acknowledged a free native, and by this right he claimed his portion of land in the community. He was affected with respect to legal process in his collateral affinities through nine degrees. For instance, every murder committed had a fine levied on the relations of the murderer divided into nine degrees, his brother paying the greatest and the ninth in affinity the least amount. This fine was distributed in the same way among the relatives of the victim. A person past the ninth degree of descent formed a new family. Every family was represented by its elder, and these elders from every family were delegates of the National Council."

Bearing upon the same subject Wilkins writes : " Welsh names pronounced by the English gradually became corrupted or modified. Thus Iorwerth was transmuted into Edward, Gwilym into William, Ieuan into John and Jones, Evan into Evans, Ricart into Richard, Rhodri into Roderick, Owain into Owen, Gruffydd into Griffith, and Dafydd into David or Davies." Which is a curious way of putting the matter, since these names were mostly borrowed from the Bible or from the English or Norman-French. It would be more correct to say that Welsh names were transmuted or reconverted according to their origin. " But here we have the immediate origin of Jones, Williams, Richards, Griffiths, Roderick, and Edwards. By the same process Ap Harry [*i.e.*, the son of Harry] became Parry; Ap Robert, Probert; Ap Richard, Prichard; and Ap Howell, Powell; while Vychan became Vaughan. Piers was possibly the Norman original of Pearce, and Stephen of Stephens, Reynalt of Reynolds, etc. The change is stated to have occurred in the middle of the sixteenth century. Our authority is *Ellis's Letters*, in which valuable repository of old correspondence the following note appears: Robert Lee, Bishop of Lichfield, and in 1535 President of the Marches of Wales, was the first who abridged the long names of the Welsh gentry. Wearied with their numberless *aps*, he ordered the last name to be retained." Pennant, in his *Tour in Wales*, describes the circumstances in his account of Tre Mostyn: " Before I quit the house," he says, " I must take notice that Thomas ap Richard, ap Howel, ap Ievan Vychan, Lord of Mostyn, and his brother Piers, founder of the family of Trelaere, were the first who abridged their name, and that on the following occasion: In the reign of Henry VIII Lee sat at one of the courts on a Welsh cause, and wearied with the quantity of *aps* in the jury, directed that the panel should assume the last name or that of their residence, and that Thomas ap Richard, ap Howell, ap Ievan Vychan should for the future be reduced to the poor dissyllable Mostyn, no doubt to the great mortification of many an ancient line."

At the battle of Brynglas between Owain Glyndwr and Mortimer, Welshwomen were accused of so misconducting themselves that Henry issued an express law forbidding any Englishman to marry a Welshwoman. Westmoreland conveys the tidings to the King in the opening scene of the first act of *Henry IV.*, Part I., when he tells how to the Council—

> There came
> A post from Wales, loaden with heavy news;
> Whose worst was,—that the noble Mortimer,
> Leading the men of Herefordshire to fight
> Against the irregular and wild Glendower,
> Was by the rude hands of that Welshman taken,
> And a thousand of his people butchered:
> Upon whose dead corpse there was such misuse,
> Such beastly shameless transformation,
> By those Welshmen done, as may not be,
> Without much shame, re-told or spoken of.
>     *K. Hen.* It seems, then, that the tidings of this broil
> Brake off our business for the Holy Land.

Pennant, referring to this accusation, cites an author who, writing near the time of the battle, says that these barbarities were committed by one

Rhys ap Grych, a follower of Glyndwr, probably excited to madness by the fury of the contest, wherein each side fought with the greatest desperation. "The barbarity," says Wilkins, "was inexcusable, but it was unjustifiable to malign a nation for the fault of one man."

Shakespeare, it may be mentioned, had the incident from Holinshed, who described it in the following words:

"Owen Glendouer, according to his accustomed manner robbing and spoiling within the English borders, caused all the forces of the shire of Hereford to assemble togither against them under the conduct of Edmund Mortimer, earle of March. By coming to trie the matter by battell, whether by treason or otherwise, so it fortuned that the English power was discomfited, the earle taken prisoner, and aboue a thousand of his people slaine in the place. The shamefull villanie vsed by the Welshwomen towards the dead carcasses was such as honest eares would be ashamed to heare and continent toongs to speake thereof. The dead bodies might not be buried without great summes of monie giuen for libertie to conueie them awaie."

Whether Shakespeare credited this report or otherwise, he did not allow it to affect his judgment of the Welsh character, as indicated by his subsequent tributes to the courage, and affability, and generosity of Owen Glendower. And as regards the incident breaking off Henry's " business for the Holy Land," Welshmen have since atoned for the interruption by the gallant part which they played in 1917-18, when they pursued the pagans—

> In those holy fields,
> Over whose acres walked those blessed feet,
> Which, fourteen hundred years ago, were nail'd
> For our advantage on the bitter cross.
>           (*Henry IV.*, Part I., Act I., Scene 1.)

There is no visible connection between *Hamlet* and Wales, yet we are reminded of the old Welsh Plygain by the following lines in *Hamlet*, which are spoken after the disappearance of the ghost :

> *Marcellus.* It faded at the crowing of the cock.
> Some say that ever 'gainst that season comes,
> Wherein our Saviour's birth is celebrated,
> The bird of dawning singeth all night long;
> And then, they say, no spirit can walk abroad,
> The nights are wholesome; then no planets strike,
> No fairy takes, nor witch hath power to harm,
> So hallowed and so gracious is the time.

The *Plygain* is the offering of public prayers and singing of carols in the Welsh churches, at cockcrow, on Christmas morning. The etymology of the word is Plu-gan, " the feathered one's song," or cock crowing.

Falstaff and the hostess both mention Wales in

the first part of *King Henry IV.*, Warwick speaks
of the " loving Welshmen " in the third part of
*King Henry VI.* (Act II., Scene 1), and Salisbury
of the " trusty Welshman " in *Richard II.* (Act II.,
Scene 4).

It is probable that many Welsh words found
their way across the border as far afield as Warwickshire, while some may have lingered there from
British times. *Kecksies* are the dry hollow stalks
of hemlock and similar plants. In *King Henry V.*
(V. 2) Burgundy uses the word—

> And nothing teems
> But hateful docks, rough thistles, kecksies, burs,
> Losing both beauty and utility.

The word (Dyer thinks) is derived from the Welsh
*cecys*, which is applied to several plants of the
umbelliferous kind.

It may be thought that a reference to *Macbeth*
is out of place in a book on " Shakespeare and the
Welsh." But the Cymry are, after all, only one
branch of the Celtic race in these islands; so that
the divergence is perhaps excusable.

Here, again, Shakespeare was indebted to Holinshed's *Chronicles of England, Scotland, and Ireland.*
There is a theory that he must also have referred
to an adaptation of *Bellendon's History.* This
adaptation, Verity says, was made by a certain

Master William Stewart at the command of Margaret, Tudor Queen of Scotland, for her son James V. Stewart's chronicle was unpublished, but it is suggested that James I. of England would have had a copy of it in manuscript, and may possibly have lent it to Shakespeare's company, which stood high in the royal favour, so that the players might compare it with Holinshed. The theory is so entirely conjectural, however, that it has failed to receive substantial support, and as far as the leading Shakespearian commentators are concerned Holinshed holds the field alone. Boas, in a very fine criticism of the tragedy, makes an interesting reference to its Celtic source. " Shakespeare," he says, " pierced, with an intuition that in an Elizabethan Englishman was wellnigh miraculous, into the very heart of Highland romance. The desolate, storm-swept heaths, where the evil powers of earth and sky may fittingly meet and greet in hideous carnival; the lonely castles, where passions of primeval intensity find their natural home, and where at dead of night murder may stealthily move to its design; the eerie atmosphere, where the hoarse croak of the raven and the scream of the owl, the fatal bellman, foretell the impending doom, and where the wraith of the victim stalks to the head of the board in the assassin's banquet-

94

ting hall; every detail is steeped in the peculiar genius of Celtic Scotland. Hitherto this fertile poetic material had found its chief expression in ballads of weird imaginative power, but these, though of supreme excellence in their kind, were only *Volkslieder*, and had no more than a local circulation. But now Shakespeare claimed for universal purposes what had hitherto been the monopoly of the clans. His mighty art preserved all the mysticism and elemental passion of the Highland story while investing it with a stupendous moral significance of which its Celtic originators had never dreamed."

Whether Shakespeare visited Scotland is not known, just as it is not known whether he visited Wales, but there is a possibility of his having done so, with a company of players, in 1601, just as he might, as Professor Boyesen tells us, have visited Elsinore with them.

In Act III., Scene 3 of *Macbeth*, where Banquo and Fleance are assailed by the murderers, Banquo is slain, but Fleance escapes. On this latter episode Malone makes the following comment: " Fleance, after the assassination of his father, fled into Wales, where by the daughter of the Prince of that country he had a son named Walter, who afterwards became Lord High Steward of Scotland, and from thence assumed the name of Walter Steward. From him in a direct line King James I. descended, in compliment to whom our author has chosen to describe Banquo, who was equally concerned with Macbeth in the murder of Duncan, as innocent of that crime."

Banquo and Fleance have been proved to be fictitious characters. They were the creatures of the imagination of the old chroniclers, but the suggestion that Shakespeare, being influenced by this account of the ancestry of James I., modified the original story to the extent of depicting Banquo as innocent of complicity in the crime is plausible if incapable of proof.

It is apparently accepted by Sir Sidney Lee, who writes: " The dramatist lavished his sympathy on Banquo, James's [supposed] ancestor, while Macbeth's vision of kings who carry ' twofold balls and treble sceptres ' plainly adverted to the Union of Scotland with England and Ireland under James's sway."

So much for Shakespeare's Welsh or Celtic plots. Of allusions to Wales or the Welsh in his plays there is more to be said. In the first part of the play of *King Henry IV.* we have some amusing comments upon Welsh character, in the person of Owen Glendower, from the lips of Hotspur. Among

96

other remarks is a reply to Glendower's claim to supernatural knowledge: " I think there's no man speaks better Welsh." Hotspur did not intend this to be a compliment, but in the opinion of Welshmen it is one of the highest that could have been paid to the Welsh chieftain. Great is the pride of the Welsh in their language. We all know Welsh to be a language of extreme antiquity; but if we believed the patriotic scholars of the past, we should be inclined to suppose that Welsh must have been spoken in the Garden of Eden and the Ark. The Rev. Thomas Richards of Coychurch, in his preface to *A British or Welsh Dictionary*, written in 1751, says of the Welsh tongue: " We hitherto not only enjoy the true name of our ancestors, but have preserved entire and uncorrupted for the most part (without any notable change or mixture with any other tongue) that Primitive Language spoken as well by the ancient Gauls as Britons some thousands of years ago. The learned Abbot Pezron mentions this with admiration, and counts it a matter of great honour to us. 'The language of the Titans,' saith he, 'which is that of the ancient Gauls, is after a revolution of above four thousand years preserved even to our time, a strange thing that so ancient a language should now be spoken by the Armorican

Britons of France and by the Britons of Wales. These are the people who have the honour to preserve the language of the posterity of Gomer, Japhet's eldest son, and the nephew of Shem, the language of those princes called Saturn and Jupiter who passed for great Deities amongst the Ancients. And as this language has continued for such a long series of ages past, so we have no reason to doubt but that the Divine Will is that it be preserved to the end of time, as we have the word of God most elegantly and faithfully translated into it. . . .'

"I know too well there are some who have such an aversion to their mother tongue that they profess a hearty desire of seeing it entirely abolished, that no remains of it may be left in this Island, so great an eyesore is the language of their forefathers become unto them. But I shall neither regard nor value what opinion such persons may have of the work, since their prejudice and ignorance render them altogether unfit to pass a right judgment upon it. Let them talk what they will of the decrease and dwindling away of the Welsh tongue, and forebode that in a few ages it will be quite driven out of Wales. Yet I shall look upon that old Welsh gentleman as the truer prophet who, being asked by Henry II., King of England, what he thought of the strength of the Welsh and of his royal expedition against them, made his answer in these words: ' This nation may suffer much, and may be in a great measure ruined, or at least weakened, O King, by your present and other future attempts, as well as formerly it hath often been, but we assure ourselves that it will never be wholly ruined by the anger or power of any mortal man unless the anger of Heaven concur to its destruction. Nor (whatever changes may happen to the other parts of the world) can I believe that any other nation or language besides the Welsh shall answer at the Great Day before the Supreme Judge for the greater part of this corner of the world.' "

Such a defence would be needless in these days of the annual Eistedfodd.

Another remark of Hotspur's in this play is interesting, as suggesting that Shakespeare was familiar with the old Welsh proverbs. Speaking of Glendower, he complains (Act III., Scene 1) that he is " as tedious as a tired horse, a railing wife, worse than a smoky house." Now there is an old Welsh proverb which Vaughan translates thus:

> Three things will drive a man from home,
> A roof that leaks,
> A house that reeks,
> A wife who scolds whene'er she speaks.

99

Fluellen, in his conversation with King Henry V. before Agincourt (*Henry V.*, Act IV., Scene 7), reminds His Majesty of the tradition that at the Battle of Creçy Captain Cadwgan Voel called to the Welsh desiring them to put leeks in their helmets, to distinguish them in the surge of battle, he having led the Welsh contingent into a field of leeks. But as a matter of fact it really is not known how the leek came to be regarded as a national emblem. One tradition states that its use originated at the battle of Meigen, fought in the seventh century between the Angles under Edwin and the British led by Cadwallon. Another version is that on St. David's birthday, A.D. 540, a great victory was obtained by the Welsh under King Arthur over the Saxon invaders, and that, by the order of St. David, the Welsh soldiers were distinguished by leeks worn in their caps.

There is no reference made to the leek as the national emblem of Wales in the works of any writer before Shakespeare, but twelve years after the date of Shakespeare's *King Henry V.*, Drayton, in his *Polyolbion* IV., describes St. David as living in the valley Ewias, amid the Hatterill Hills in Monmouthshire. It was here " that reverend British saint to contemplation lived,"

And did so truly fast.
He did only drink what crystal Hodney yields,
And fed upon the leeks he gathered in the fields,
In memory of whom, in the revolving year,
The Welshmen, on his day, the sacred herb do wear.

Meyrick thinks that, as the national colours were white and green, the leek was selected and venerated on account of its exhibiting these two colours, a theory which may be held to gain support from the fact that the daffodil is often held to be St. David's emblem. Owen Rhoscomyl gives the following explanation: Henry VII., in exile, remembered that the bards were for ever proclaiming anew the old prophecies that a Cymro should yet wear the crown of Britain. By stealth he came to Wales to stir up his countrymen to realise the old dream of deliverance, and he succeeded.

In two places we get track of him in this wandering. In Mostyn Hall the window is still shown through which he escaped to the mountains while the troops of Richard were hammering at the door to take him. At Corsygedol, in Ardudwy, the same chance favoured him, and he set sail for Brittany again from Barmouth, all his plans laid and his friends ready. It was during this wandering that the seed of our national emblem was sown. As grandson of Catherine of Valois, Harry Tudor used the green and white of Valois in his coat of arms. As a sign to each other his partisans used the green and white for a test. They did not carry it about with them. If they met each other in the field they simply pulled up a blade of grass, a wild hyacinth, a daffodil—anything that showed a green stem and a white root. If they met in a house they could lift a leek or an onion or any other vegetable which showed the two colours. And so we wear the leek, or scorn it for the daffodil, in forgetful remembrance of that day.

At the installation of the Prince of Wales at Carnarvon in July, 1911, the daffodil was substituted for the leek, and the Welsh Insurance Commissioners have also decided to prefer the dainty flower above the humble vegetable. A fierce controversy raged around this substitution, and Mr. Llewelyn Williams, K.C., M.P., entered the lists as the chief champion of the flower, which is known in Wales as *Ceninen Pedr*. In an article in *Wales* (March, 1913) he contended that " in the good old days " before the Protestant Reformation, when the native saints of Wales and a few foreign saints of world-wide fame were honoured in our Welsh churches, a festival was assigned to the chairing of St. Peter. In the old Welsh Calendars the day was marked as " Pedr Gadeiriol." It was necessary, therefore (writes Mr. Williams), to decorate the churches with flowers on that day. Now there were no artificial flowers to be bought in Wales a thousand years ago; nor could our rude forefathers obtain exotic blossoms and hothouse plants. They therefore had to gather whatever wild flowers were in bloom at that time of the year and use them for the decoration of churches on the feast-day of " Pedr Gadeiriol." That is how and why the daffodil came to be used on these occasions, and that is why it is still known in some parts of Wales as " Ceninen Pedr." But why " Ceninen " ? Why should it be called " The Leek of Peter " ? Because the daffodil is of the same species as the leek. What rhythm is to prose the daffodil is to the leek. It is the leek transformed, made beautiful, etherealised, transplanted into the odour of sanctity. But how did the daffodil, Peter's Leek, come to be associated with St. David ? How did it come to be known as " Blodyn Dewi " ? This again opens up a very interesting field of inquiry, and I am greatly indebted to my friend, Mr. Griffith, the erudite Vicar of Llangynwyd, for the true answer. Dewi was canonised by his countrymen either during his lifetime or shortly afterwards. All over South Wales churches were dedicated to him. But the ancient British Church was not at the time in communion with Rome, and it was not till the twelfth century, 500 years or so after his death, that Dewi Sant was canonised by the Roman authorities. It would be too tedious to set out here in detail how, after the reform of the calendar, St. David's Day and " Pedr Gadeiriol " came to fall on the same day—viz., March 1st. My friend, Mr. Griffith, has worked it out most ingeniously and convincingly, and I merely summarise the result of his labour. And so the daffodil, being used for decorating the churches on Dygwyl Dewi Sant, came to be known, not only as " Ceninen Pedr," but also as " Blodyn Dewi."

Had we been living in the Middle Ages, it is possible that this controversy would have developed into a war of the Leek and the Daffodil, and foremost among the champions of the Leek might have been found that mediæval monarch whose fifteenth century effigy in stone (preserved in the crypt of Worcester Cathedral) holds proudly in its hand not one, but two leeks !

In reply to Fluellen's sarcastically polite demand that he should eat the leek, which he had despised (*Henry V.*, Act V., Scene 1), Pistol fiercely ejaculates, " Not for Cadwaladr and all his goats." Shakespeare evidently knew something of Cadwaladr's partiality for goats. Now this is a very interesting point which proves that Shakespeare was well versed in the legends of Wales. What precise version of the history of that goat-owning and goat-loving monarch he was familiar with we do not know; but the reader may be interested in an account of one of his adventures as related by Wirt Sikes in his *British Goblins*:

" Cadwaladr owned a very handsome goat named Jenny, of which he was extremely fond, and which seemed equally fond of him, and one day, as if the very *diawl* possessed her, she ran away into the hills, with Cadwaladr tearing after her, half mad with anger and affright. At last his Welsh blood got so hot, as the goat eluded him again and again, that he flung a stone at her, which knocked her over a precipice, and she fell bleating to her doom. Cadwaladr made his way to the foot of the crag; the goat was dying, but not dead, and licked his hand, which so affected the poor man that he burst into tears, and, sitting on the ground, took the goat's head on his arm. The moon rose, and still he sat there. Presently he found that the goat had become transformed into a beautiful young woman, whose brown eyes, as her head lay on his arm, looked into his in a very disturbing way. ' Ah, Cadwaladr,' said she; ' have I found you ?'

" Now Cadwaladr had a wife at home, and was

much discomforted by these singular circumstances, and when the goat—*yn awr*, maiden—arose and, putting her black slipper on the end of a moonbeam, held out her hand to him, he put his hand in hers and went with her. As for the hand, though it looked so fair, it felt just like a hoof. They were soon at the top of the highest mountain in Wales, and surrounded by a vapoury company of goats with shadowy horns. These raised a most unearthly bleating about his ears. One, which seemed to be king, had a voice that sounded above the din, as the castle bells of Carmarthen used to do long ago above the other bells of the town. This one rushed at Cadwaladr, and, butting him in the stomach, sent him toppling over the crag as he had sent the poor nanny-goat. When he came to himself after his fall the morning sun was shining on him, and the birds were singing over his head. But he saw no more of either his goat or the fairy she had turned into from that time to his death."

Goats were held in Wales in peculiar esteem for their supposed possession of occult intellectual powers. They were regarded as being on good terms with the *Tylwyth Teg* (the fairy family), who combed their beards out every Friday night to make them presentable for the Sabbath.

An interesting discovery is claimed by Mr. H. C.

Hart in the *Arden Shakespeare*. He has found in the Quarto of the *Merry Wives of Windsor* what he believes to be the only Welsh phrase ever attempted by Shakespeare. Sir Hugh Evans's valedictory greeting to mine Host of the Garter (Act IV., Scene 5) is " Fare you well." On this, Mr. Hart makes the following comment:

" Instead of ' Fare you well ' the Quarto has ' Grate why, mine host.' I have not seen any note on the words *grate why*. No doubt they are Welsh, and the letter *r* is a misprint. They mean ' bless you ' or ' preserve you ' (*cadw chwi*), as I judge from the expression *Du cat a whee* (God keep you), which is dealt with by Nares. . . . It is pleasant, if I am right, to find one Welsh expression in Evans's mouth—the only one, I believe, in Shakespeare. From the position of the words at the close of the speech it seems to me there can be no doubt they were his valediction."

Mr. Hart also points out that in the remark of Dr. Caius, " He is pray his Bible well " (alluding to Sir Hugh's absence), the word Bible is used for the only time in Shakespeare, whose other references are to " The Word " and " Holy Writ."

Sir Hugh Evans, in the *Merry Wives of Windsor*, mentions Metheglin. Queen Elizabeth is said to have been fond of this ancient British drink.

" ' Metheglin,' is derived from the Welsh Medey-glin, and spoken of by Howell, who was clerk to the Privy Council in 1640. The recipe for Metheglin is as follows: To nine gallons of boiling water put twenty-eight pounds of honey, add the peel of three lemons with a small quantity of ginger, mace, cloves, and rosemary. When it is quite cold add two tablespoonfuls of yeast. Put this in a cask and allow it to ferment; at the expiration of six months bottle it off for use" (*Cups and their Customs*, London, 1863).

Metheglin (pronounced metheg-lin) is still made and drunk in various parts of Wales. *Medd*, from which we have the English name of metheglin —*i.e.*, mead—is a Welsh word denoting honey.

An allusion to Carnarvonshire appears in Act II., Scene 3 of *Henry VIII*. The passage, which is as follows, occurs between the old Lady and Anne Boleyn, the mother of Queen Elizabeth:

> *Anne.* How dare you talk !
> I swear again I would not be a queen
> For all the world.
>    *Old Lady.*       In faith, for little England
> You'ld venture an emballing [investment with the crown
>     and sceptre]. I myself
> Would for Carnarvonshire, although there 'longed
> No more to the crown than that.

Commentators have debated the point as to what Shakespeare meant by " little England."

Whalley and Stevens suggested that the term referred to Pembrokeshire, " the little England beyond Wales "—not unreasonably, perhaps, as it may be supposed that the proposal to make Anne Marchioness of Pembroke was known to the two women. It seems to us, however, that the comparison is clearly between little England and the big world.

A character in the same play has been made the subject of some interesting speculations. Lord Mostyn, we are told, has in his collection of Welsh manuscripts a treatise on *Henry VIII. and his Times*. The author was one Ellis Griffith, who described himself as " A soldier of Calais." It is suggested that this historian is identical with the Griffith of whom Queen Catherine said:

> After my death I wish no other herald,
> No other speaker of my living actions,
> To keep mine honour from corruption,
> But such an honest chronicler as Griffith.

Mr. Pym Yeatman, however (*The Gentle Shakespeare*), identifies this character with Griffin, who, he states, was of Welsh descent, and an actual cousin of Shakespeare. But it does not seem very clear why Shakespeare should have confused the name of his own kinsman.

To leave the Histories for the Comedies awhile:

in *Much Ado about Nothing* is a dialogue of which the following is a fragment:

> *Beatrice.* By my troth, I am exceeding ill: hey ho !
> *Margaret.* For a hawk, a horse, or a husband ?
> *Beatrice.* For the letter that begins them all, H.
>
> (Act III., Scene 4.)

Hunter (*New Illustrations*) suggests that the H. may have stood for Herbert (see Chapter XIV.), and adds that, as individual persons were sometimes introduced on the Elizabethan stage, it should be " no matter for surprise if we find that the character of a young nobleman of those times is partially reflected in the character of Benedick, and that certain events in the history of that young nobleman's life were the immediate occasion of the writing these scenes of the drama." Hunter alludes to William Herbert, the third Earl of Pembroke, whose disinclination to marriage was the cause of much regret to his literary and other friends, and is supposed to have inspired some of the earlier numbers in Shakespeare's *Sonnets*. Hunter returns to the subject in his explanation of Pistol's challenge (*Henry IV.*, Part II., Act V., Scene 3): " Under which king, Bezonian ? Speak or die !" The word " Bezonian," he explains, was used in the army for " a raw soldier, unexpert in his weapon and other military points." It is thus explained by Barret in his *Theorike and Practike of Modern Warres*, dedicated to Lord Herbert. Hunter adds: "The dedication to Lord Herbert of a work on this subject is a proof additional to those already produced of the young lord's military ardour, one of the points in which he resembles Benedick." It is not fanciful, knowing what we do of Mary Fitton, the "Dark Lady of the Sonnets," to regard Benedick and Beatrice as portraits, no doubt idealised, and in one case perhaps half unconscious, of Herbert and Mary Fitton.

One of the "doubtful" plays associated with the name of Shakespeare was *The Birth of Merlin*. It was first issued by Francis Kirkman in 1662, and the title page describes it as having been "written by William Shakespeare and William Rowley." Among the characters of this rather extravagant romance are an Earl of Cornwall, an Earl of Gloucester, and a courtier Oswald. These names are all familiar to the student of Shakespeare, so that it might be worth while to examine the title of this play more closely. Another of the Shakespeare apocryphal plays is *Locrine*, the theme of which is taken from Geoffrey of Monmouth.

# CHAPTER VIII.

## THE WELSH CAPTAIN IN *KING RICHARD II.*

Of the Welsh soldiers depicted by Shakespeare in the Histories, the first is the " Captain of a Band of Welshmen " introduced into his play of *King Richard II.*, and in one portion of the play the action moves from Milford Haven to Flint. King Richard II. was strongly supported by the Welsh. His bodyguard consisted of 10,000 Welsh archers. " Sleep in peace, Dickon," was the saying of the Welsh; " we will take care of thee." His expedition to Ireland, which cost him his crown, took place in 1399. No news reached Richard of the landing of Bolingbroke, at Ravenspur in Yorkshire (now swallowed up by the sea), until a fortnight after the event. On his return the King fell into the hands of the Duke of Lancaster at Flint, as described in the play.

Richard was the son of that Black Prince for whom Welsh archers fought so bravely at Creçy. In the opening scenes of the play Bolingbroke (who afterwards becomes King Henry IV.) and Lord Mowbray are banished from the country, but subsequently, when Richard II. is in Ireland, quelling an insurrection, Bolingbroke returns and leads a revolt against the King. Richard is a weak and sentimental monarch, and no match for the masterful Bolingbroke, to whom he eventually surrenders his crown and sceptre.

*King Richard II.* was published in 1597. Its source was Holinshed's Chronicles (second edition, 1586-87), and it is worthy of note that this fact is considered proved by means of the scene in which the Welsh Captain appears. Mr. Stone tells us that many new passages were added to the first edition of Holinshed, and the omen of the withering of the bay trees was not mentioned in the first edition. But there is no mention of Richard's journey to the Holy Land in Holinshed, and it is supposed that Shakespeare must have referred to Stowe's *Annals* as well as to the invaluable Holinshed.

King Richard was expected to land in Wales from Ireland on a certain date, but failed to land at the time appointed, with disastrous results, as we may read in Holinshed:

"But when they missed the King there was a brute [*i.e.*, *bruit*, rumour] spred among them that the King was suerlie dead; which wrought such an impression and euill disposition in the minds of the Welshmen and others that for anie persuasion which the earle of Salisburie might vse they would not go foorth with him till they saw the King; onelie they were contented to stay fourteene daies to see if he should come or not; but when he came not within that tearme they would no longer abide, but scaled [*i.e.*, scattered] and departed awaie: whereas if the King had come before their breaking vp no doubt they would haue put the duke of Hereford in aduenture of a field [*i.e.*, have offered battle to him]; so that the King's lingering of time before his coming ouer gaue opportunities to the duke to bring things to pass as he could haue wished, and took from the King all occasion [*i.e.*, opportunity] to recouer afterwards anie forces sufficient to resist him.  In this yeare in a manner throughout all the realme of England *old bai trees withered*, and afterwards, contrarie to all men's thinking, grew greene again; a strange sight and supposed to import some vnknowne event."

Upon the foregoing account Shakespeare based the following scene:

### ACT II.

#### SCENE 4.—*A camp in Wales.*

*Enter* SALISBURY *and a* Welsh Captain.

*Captain.* My Lord of Salisbury, we have stayed ten days
And hardly kept our countrymen together,
And yet we hear no tidings from the King;
Therefore we will disperse ourselves: farewell.

*Salisbury.* Stay yet another day, thou trusty Welshman:
The King reposeth all his confidence in thee.
   *Captain.* 'Tis thought the King is dead: we will not stay.
The bay trees in our country are all withered,
And meteors fright the fixed stars of heaven.
The pale-faced moon looks bloody on the earth,
And lean-looked prophets whisper fearful change.
Rich men look sad, and ruffians dance and leap,
The one, in fear to lose what they enjoy,
The other to enjoy by rage and war.
These signs forerun the death or fall of Kings.
Farewell; our countrymen are gone and fled,
As well assured Richard their King is dead.   *[Exit.*

The bay-tree was, of course, symbolical of victory.
The import of its withering could not therefore
be ignored. "This enumeration of prodigies,"
says Johnson, "is in the highest degree poetical
and striking"; and Verity adds: "It imports a sense
of mystery and awe, and raises the tragedy to a
loftier plane. The very heavens are telling the
downfall of the King. Note how the speech fits
the representative of the imaginative and superstitious Celtic race."

So far the Welshmen had been loyal to the King,
and were prepared to fight for him, but they lived
in superstitious times, and feeling that the fates
had decided against Richard, or persuaded that
he was dead, they abandoned the field. The
suggestion has been made that the Welsh Captain
is intended to represent Owain Glyndwr, as Boling-

broke speaks in Act III., Scene 1 of proceeding to fight with " Glendower and his complices." In that case, however, one hardly sees why Shakespeare should have hesitated to give him a name.

On the other hand, the speech, with its allusions to withered bay-trees, meteors, a bloody moon, and other disastrous omens, is entirely in Glendower's vein.

In Scene 2 of Act III. the Welshmen have dispersed: the mercenaries to join Bolingbroke, since a live and present King is better than a dead one or an absentee; and we meet with Richard, newly landed, but a day too late, on " the coast of Wales. A castle in view." His first words set the commentator a problem. They are these: " Barkloughly Castle call they this at hand?" We shall look on the maps in vain for Barkloughly. Shakespeare found the name in Holinshed. It was probably a copyist's or printer's error for Hertlowlie, or, as we know it, Harlech.

# CHAPTER IX

## OWEN GLENDOWER

In the last act of *King Richard II.* Henry Boling-broke, who, having landed in England during Richard's absence in Ireland, has defeated the latter on his return, is overcome with remorse on hearing of the King's assassination in prison; and announces, in a closing passage, which is almost certainly not from Shakespeare's pen, but an unrevised fragment of the old pageant-play " licked into shape," by the Blackfriars dramatist, his intention of seeking absolution in a " voyage to the Holy Land." But after his accession to the throne in the first part of *King Henry IV.* this project is perforce abandoned, for there comes—

> A post from Wales loaden with heavy news,
> Whose worst was that the noble Mortimer,
> Leading the men of Herefordshire to fight
> Against the irregular and wild Glendower,
> Was by the rude hands of that Welshman taken. . . .

—lines in which we seem to read something of the fear which irregular troops, operating in familiar country, have always inspired in the leaders of conscript peasants trained in the conventional school of war.

117

To Prince Hal, in the Boar's Head Tavern, the rising is announced by Falstaff in other terms: " There's villainous news abroad . . . you must to the court in the morning. That same mad fellow of the North, Percy, and he of Wales, that gave Amamon the bastinado, and made Lucifer cuckold, and swore the devil his true liegeman upon the cross of a Welsh hook—what a plague call you him ?—Owen, Owen . . . and his son-in-law Mortimer, and old Northumberland; and that sprightly Scot of Scots, Douglas, that runs o' horseback up a hill perpendicular."

What can we make of this somewhat mysterious reference? "Amaymon, King of the East," appears in " an inventarie of the names and effects of divels and spirits," contained in R. Scott's *Discoverie of Witchcraft* (1584). But what of the " cross of a Welsh hook "? It might be suggested that neither a Welsh hook nor any other hook is in the shape of a cross, and that Falstaff's reference must be of the nature of mere fooling. Yet a little reflection seems to throw some light on the subject. It was always customary among soldiers to swear by the hilt, or cross, of a sword. To take a Welsh instance, in Dekker's *Satiro Mastrix* we have Sir Rees ap Vaughan swearing by " the crosse of this sword and dagger." Now the Welsh irregular soldiery were largely foot-soldiers and pikemen, and they fought largely against horsemen. We may be sure, therefore, that a favourite form of pike, partisan, or halberd would have been that in which part of the blade is formed as a hook, wherewith to drag heavily-armed knights or horsemen from their saddles, or to lame horses; and above this hook would be a cross-bar or blade to parry sword-strokes or the blows of another pike or partisan. Such a pike might well be known, by those whose knowledge of its uses was entirely disagreeable, " as a Welsh hook." And the bearer of such a weapon, if anxious to emphasise the truth of a statement, or solemnly to pledge his word, would be likely to imitate his superiors, and to swear upon the cross, not of his sword, but of his pike or hook. Or, what is more to the purpose, he might fairly be expected to do so by Falstaff— and by Shakespeare, who may have seen such weapons in the houses of Welsh friends.

Before proceeding to consider Shakespeare's portrait of Glendower (or Owain Glyndwr, to give him his rightful name), the intrepid champion and leader of the Welsh peasantry, it will be as well briefly to examine the historical situation as it was in fact and as it is depicted in the play.

The date of the first part of *King Henry IV.* was

1596-97, and for the groundwork of the play Shakespeare was as usual indebted to Holinshed. Henry, in his plot against Richard, had the powerful support of Henry Percy, Earl of Northumberland, his brother, Thomas, Earl of Worcester, and his son, Henry Percy, surnamed Hotspur, but having ascended the throne he was guilty of treating them with something less than proper gratitude. He thereby aroused the wrath of the Percies, who kept the Border against the Scots in addition to garrisoning the castles of North Wales. The Percies, at the battle of Homildon Hill, had taken prisoner many knights and nobles, and, according to usage, they looked forward to ransoming these prisoners as a source of gain. Henry, however, stubbornly denied them the privilege. The Percies, hotly resentful of his treatment of their reasonable demands, were given yet another cause of offence. Sir Edmund Mortimer, one of the Lord Marchers, was taken prisoner by Owain Glyndwr, and the Percies required of the King that he should ransom or otherwise cause him to be delivered out of prison. According to Holinshed, upon whose version Shakespeare or his predecessor relied, (even to confounding Sir Edmund Mortimer with Edmund Mortimer, the Earl of March), the Percies eventually went to Windsor to claim the deliverance of

Mortimer from the hands of Glendower, and he continues:

" The King, when he had studied on the matter, made answer that the Earle of March was not taken prisoner for his cause nor in his seruice, but willinglie suffered himself to be taken because he would not withstand the attempts of Owen Glendouer and his complices, and therefore he would neither ransome him or releeue him. The Persies with this answer and fradulent excuse were not a little fumed, and they departed vowing to depose the King and entered into their league with Glendouer." A " tripartite deed," continues Holinshed, " was doone (as some have said) through a foolish credit given to a vaine prophesie as though King Henrie was the moldwarpe [*i.e.*, mole] cursed of God's owne mouth, and they three were the dragon, the lion, and the woolfe, which should diuide the realme betweene them. Such is the deviation (saith Hall) and not divination of those blind and fantasticall dreames of the Welsh prophesiers."

Holinshed further tells us that the King " was not hastie to purchase the deliverance of the Earle of March because his title to the crowne was well inough knowen," and refers to Owain Glyndwr in the following words:

" About the mid of August the King to chastise

the presumptuous attempts of the Welshmen went
with a great power of men into Wales to pursue
the Capteine of the Welsh rebell Owen Glendouer,
but in effect lost his labor, for Owen conveied
himselfe out of the waie into his knowen lurking-
places, and (as was thought) through art magike
he caused such foule weather of winds, tempest,
raine, snow and haile to be raised for the annoiance
of the King's armie that the like had not beene
heard of; in such sort that the King was constrained
to returne home, hauing caused his people yet to
spoile and burne first a great part of the countrie. . . .

" . . . Edmund Mortimer, earle of March, prisoner
with Owen Glendouer, whether for irksomenesse
of cruell captivitie or feare of death or for what
other cause it is vncertaine, agreed to take part
with Owen against the King of England, and tooke
to wife the daughter of the said Owen. Strange
wonders happened (as men reported) at the
nativitie of this man, for the same night he was
borne all his father's horsses in the stable were
found to stand in bloud vp to their bellies "—a statement which will make the profane wonder upon
what system the said stables were drained.

Henry IV. found the throne a very uneasy seat.
Conspiracy and intrigue disquieted the beginnings
of his reign, and the Welsh opposition developed

into open rebellion. Well might Shakespeare make the troubled monarch say : "Uneasy lies the head that wears a crown."

To go back to the opening of the play, we find the King, as already stated, contemplating an expedition to the Holy Land, but abandoning, or at all events postponing, "his holy purpose to Jerusalem" on receipt of "the heavy news from Wales," which includes that report of the mutilation, by Welshwomen, of Mortimer's wounded, which we have already glanced at in a previous chapter. This news was immediately followed by the still "more uneven and unwelcome news" of the battle of Holmedon (Homildon), when—

> The gallant Hotspur there,
> Young Harry Percy, and brave Archibald,
> That ever-valiant and approved Scot,
> At Holmedon met,
> Where they did spend a sad and bloody hour,
> As by discharge of their artillery,
> And shape of likelihood, the news was told;
> For he that brought them, in the very heat
> And pride of their contention did take horse,
> Uncertain of the issue any way.

But this news is at once followed by the welcome report that the Scots are utterly defeated, having lost ten thousand men with "two-and-twenty knights," while among Hotspur's prisoners are Fife, the son of the Earl of Douglas, and the Earls

123

of Athol, Murray, Angus, and Monteith—news which sets the King envying Northumberland the possession of such a son.

" O," he exclaims—

> O that it could be prov'd
> That some night-tripping fairy had exchang'd
> In cradle-clothes our children where they lay,
> And call'd mine Percy, his Plantagenet !

—a passage which reminds us that the theory of the fairy changeling, although not unknown in the Anglo-Norman provinces, was essentially a Celtic superstition, as indeed it remains to this day. Nothing is more likely than that Shakespeare had heard of fairy changelings from Welsh lips—it may be from Alys Griffin herself.

The construction of this first scene is crude; the chief speakers announce the latest news in detail, although it becomes evident that they were already familiar with it. Thus, after envying Northumberland his son, Henry complains of " this young Percy's pride," in that—

> The prisoners . . .
> To his own use he keeps, and sends me word
> I shall have none but Mordake Earl of Fife.

At which Westmoreland exclaims:

> This is his uncle's teaching, this is Worcester,
> Malevolent to |you in all aspects.

" But I," says Henry—

> Have sent for him to answer this;
> And for this cause we must awhile neglect
> Our holy purpose to Jerusalem.

Which purpose, as a matter of fact, he had previously stated was broken off by the tidings of
the " broil " with Glendower.

Scene 3 shows us Hotspur, Worcester, and
Northumberland arraigned by Henry. Worcester,
having hinted at his services in making Henry's
greatness " so portly," is promptly dismissed
the Court. Northumberland explains that the
prisoners taken at Holmedon—

> Were . . . not with such strength denied
> As was delivered to your majesty.
> Either envy, therefore, or misprision [misunderstanding]
> Is guilty of this fault, and not my son.

To which Hotspur adds that he " did deny no
prisoners," but that when " dry with rage and
extreme toil, breathless and faint after the battle,"

> Came there a certain lord, neat and trimly dress'd,
> Fresh as a bridegroom, and his chin new-reap'd
> Show'd like a stubble-land at harvest-home.
> He was perfumed like a milliner,
> And 'twixt his finger and his thumb he held
> A pouncet-box, which ever and anon
> He gave his nose, and took't away again.

In short, another Osric, whom Hotspur loves
rather less than Hamlet loved the " waterfly."

Having further irritated the rough-and-ready Northcountryman by chiding the soldiers who were bearing the dead from the field for bringing—

> A slovenly unhandsome corse
> Betwixt the wind and his nobility,

he demands Percy's prisoners on behalf of the King. Hotspur, " all smarting with his wounds, being cold to be so pestered with a popinjay," answers:

> Neglectingly, I know not what,
> He should, or he should not; for he made me mad,
> To see him shine so brisk, and smell so sweet,
> And talk so like a waiting-gentlewoman,
> Of guns and drums and wounds . . . and but for these vile guns
> He would himself have been a soldier.

The upshot of which is that the hater of " villanous saltpetre " gets no satisfaction out of Hotspur, who probably indulged himself in a much more vigorous and racy reply than either the popinjay or himself cared to repeat to Henry.

Henry, however, is not to be pacified; Hotspur offers him his prisoners even now only on the condition " that we " (the King is speaking)—

> shall ransom straight
> His brother-in-law, the foolish Mortimer;
> Who, on my soul, hath wilfully betray'd
> The lives of those that he did lead to fight
> Against that great magician, damn'd Glendower,

> Whose daughter, as we hear, the Earl of March
> Hath lately married.  Shall our coffers, then,
> Be emptied to redeem a traitor home ? . . .
> No, on the barren mountains let him starve. . . .

Henry, be it remarked, already had experience of those "barren mountains," and was to have more.

Here already we have some evidence of the dread in which Glendower is held.

The Earl of Westmoreland (Act I., Scene 1) speaks of the Welsh chieftain as "the irregular and wild Glendower," but to the King, who has already had a foretaste of his powers of opposition, he is "the great magician, damn'd Glendower." But Hotspur, in his instant defence of "Mortimer," pays a handsome tribute to the prowess of the Welshman.

> Revolted Mortimer !
> He never did fall off, my sovereign liege,
> But by the chance of war; to prove that true,
> Needs no more but one tongue for all those wounds,
> Those mouthéd wounds, which valiantly he took,
> When, on the gentle Severn's sedgy bank,
> In single opposition, hand to hand,
> He did confound the best part of an hour
> In changing hardiment, with great Glendower.
> Three times they breathed and three times did they drink,
> Upon agreement, of swift Severn's flood,
> Who then, affrighted by their bloody looks,
> Ran fearfully among the trembling reeds,
> And hid his crisp head in the hollow bank,
> Blood-stainéd with these valiant combatants.

But the King refuses to accept Hotspur's version of the matter, saying:

> Thou dost belie him, Percy, thou dost belie him;
> He never did encounter with Glendower:
> I tell thee,
> He durst as well have met the devil alone
> As Owen Glendower for an enemy.

Which argues a remarkable respect for the occult powers of Glendower, or a very poor opinion of Mortimer's courage.

Dismissed from Court with a threat and the summary order to surrender their prisoners, the now disaffected Worcester and Hotspur seek the assistance of Glendower and Mortimer, and the tripartite plot to dethrone the King is devised.

At the time when Owain Glyndwr figured in Welsh history, a fierce struggle was being waged between the bards and the friars. The friars had fallen into degenerate ways, while the bards represented the rising national spirit. Owain Glyndwr, who sided with the bards, had retired to his beautiful dwelling at Sycharth after the abdication of Richard II. Here he assembled the Welsh poets and minstrels, and we may picture him, at this period, seated in the bosom of his family, listening with delight to the rhapsodies of the bards as they told of the prowess of his ancestors—the Princes of Powis. Glyndwr's home at Sycharth is described with much minuteness by Owen's bard, Iolo Goch : " Encircled with a moat filled with water, the entrance to this Baron's Palace, this mansion of generosity, the magnificent habitation of the chief Lord of Powys, is a costly gate. . . . A Neapolitan building of eighteen apartments, a fair timber structure on the summit of a green hill, reared towards heaven on four admirable pilasters." Attached to the mansion were orchards and vineyards, while herds of deer fed in the park. " Loudly chanted the bards the praises of Glyndwr, and many a fine heroic ' Cowydd ' preserves the memory of his deeds and the admiration of his people. A comet appeared in 1402, and was hailed as a great augury for Glyndwr. Iolo Goch became so excited in his fervour thereat as to throw himself open to the charge of positive blasphemy " (Wilkins).

Glyndwr was a fervid patriot, and the dream of his life was to secure the independence of his native country, reform the Welsh Church, and establish two Universities, one in North and one in South Wales. By personal inclination he was a musician and a poet; by force of circumstances he became a warrior, for, being roused to anger by the tyranny and arrogance of the English Lords of the Marches, he headed a revolt of the suffering peasantry, was acclaimed the new Prince of Wales, and actually established a Parliament at Dolgelly and Machynlleth, sending his ambassadors to the French Court.

In Shakespeare's play Glendower makes his first appearance in a striking scene which represents a conference between Hotspur, Worcester, Mortimer, and himself, in a room in the Archdeacon's house at Bangor. The subject under discussion is a " tripartite deed " for the division of the kingdom should the revolt against the King succeed. Wales " beyond the Severn shore " has been set apart as Glendower's portion. At the very start of the conference Hotspur, the haughty, quick-tempered, but practical Englishman, falls foul of the mystical Glendower. " At my nativity," declares Glendower, with the naïve egoism of the Celt,

> The front of heaven was full of fiery shapes,
> Of burning cressets; and at my birth,
> The frame and huge foundation of the earth,
> Shak'd like a coward.

*Hotspur.* Why so it would have done at the same season, if your mother's cat had but kittened, though yourself had never been born.

*Glendower.* I say the earth did shake when I was born.

*Hotspur.* And I say the earth was not of my mind,
If you suppose as fearing you it shook.

> *Glendower.* The heavens were all on fire, the earth did tremble.

" O, then the earth shook to see the heavens on fire, and not in fear of your nativity," says

Hotspur, and proceeds to give a humorous dis-
quisition upon the nature of earthquakes:

> Diseased nature oftentimes breaks forth
> In strange eruptions: oft the teeming earth
> Is with a kind of cholic pinch'd and vex'd
> By the imprisoning of unruly wind
> Within her womb; which, for enlargement striving,
> Shakes the old beldame earth, and topples down
> Steeples, and moss-grown towers.  At your birth,
> Our grandam earth, having this distemperature,
> In passion shook.

This is too much for Glendower, who had already
hinted that Hotspur's incredulity and levity were
offensive to him.

> *Glend.*           Cousin, of many men
> I do not bear these crossings.  Give me leave
> To tell you once again,—that at my birth,
> The front of heaven was full of fiery shapes;
> The goats ran from the mountains, and the herds
> Were strangely clamorous to the frighted fields.
> These signs have mark'd me extraordinary;
> And all the courses of my life do show,
> I am not in the roll of common men.
> Where is he living,—clipp'd in with the sea
> That chides the banks of England, Scotland, Wales,
> Which calls me pupil, or hath read to me ?
> And bring him out, that is but woman's son,
> Can trace me in the tedious ways of art,
> And hold me pace in deep experiments.

" I think there is no man speaks better Welsh,"
retorts Hotspur  dryly: by  which, presumably,

he means " better gibberish." " I will to dinner."
Mortimer speaks a word of warning:

> Peace, cousin Percy; you will make him mad.
>   *Glend.* I can call spirits from the vasty deep.
>   *Hot.* Why, so can I; or so can any man:
> But will they come, when you do call for them ?
>   *Glend.* Why, I can teach you, cousin, to command
> The devil.
>   *Hot.* And I can teach thee, coz, to shame the devil,
> By telling truth. Tell truth, and shame the devil.
> If thou have power to raise him, bring him hither,
> And I'll be sworn, I have power to shame him hence. . . .

Glendower displays a curious characteristic,
which is often met with in men possessed of set
ideas; while sometimes irascible and taking offence
at every word, at other times, when pursuing a
train of thought, he is completely oblivious of
what is said to him. Mortimer, fearing an explo-
sion, breaks in hastily:

> Come, come,
> No more of this unprofitable chat.

But Glendower, for once, has not taken offence;
pursuing the argument of his greatness, he tells
how thrice he has defeated Henry Bolingbroke
and sent him " bootless home and weather-beaten
back."

In spite of another indiscreet witticism, he has
restored his equanimity by demonstrating his

greatness as magician and soldier, and settles down to business in perfect good humour. " Come, here's the map," he says.

> Shall we divide our right
> According to our threefold order ta'en ?

But Hotspur, on hearing the provisions of the " tripartite deed " drawn up by the Archdeacon of Bangor, declares that his moiety, to the north of the Trent, does not in quantity equal the others, and the quarrel between the imperious Anglo-Norman and the fiery Celt breaks out afresh.

> *Hotspur.* I'll have it so, a little charge [change ?] will do it.
> *Glendower.* I will not have it altered.
> *Hotspur.*                                   Will not you ?
> *Glendower.* No, nor you shall not.
> *Hotspur.*                               Who shall say me nay ?
> *Glendower.* Why, that will I.
> *Hotspur.*                           Let me not understand you then;
> Speak it in Welsh.

An unfortunate speech to make to any Celt; for the Celt is quickly roused by scornful criticism, and the Welshman, wrongly thinking that Hotspur is casting a slur upon his mastery of English, is at once up in arms again.

> *Glendower.* I can speak English, lord, as well as you,
> For I was trained up in the English Court,
> Where, being young, I framéd to the harp,
> Many an English ditty lovely well,
> And gave my tongue a helpful ornament,
> A virtue that was never seen in you.

In which we see something of Glendower's love of, and respect for poetry, music, and scholarship, and his secret contempt for the rude unlettered Englishman. Hotspur's reply is the usual retort of ignorance.

> Marry, I'm glad of it with all my heart.
> I had rather be a kitten and cry mew
> Than one of these same metre ballad-mongers.
> I had rather hear a brazen canstick turned,*
> And that would set my teeth nothing on edge,
> Nothing so much as mincing poetry.

At which Glendower seems to give up this fore-runner of the typical public-schoolboy as hopeless, for, suddenly changing the subject he says good-humouredly, as one might to a fractious child: "Come, you shall have Trent turn'd."

Holinshed, again, is Shakespeare's authority for Glendower's claim that he was reared in the English Court:

" This Owen Glendouer was sonne of an esquier of Wales named Griffith Vichan: he dwelled in the parish of Conwaie within the countie of Merioneth in North Wales in a place called Glin-dourwie, which is as much as to saie in English as the Vallie by the side of the water of the Dee,

---

* The reference is presumably to the grating, chattering shriek of brass turned on a primitive lathe.

by occasion whereof he was surnamed Glindour Dew.

" He was first set to studie the lawes of the realme and became an vtter barrester or an apprentise of the law (as they terme him), and serued King Richard at Flint Castell, when he was taken by Henrie, duke of Lancaster, though others have written that he serued this King Henrie the fourth before he came to atteine the crown in roome of an esquier."

When Glendower leaves the room to bring in Lady Mortimer and Lady Percy, Mortimer takes advantage of his absence to expostulate with Hotspur on his constant crossing of his father-in-law. " Fie, cousin Percy ! how you cross my father !" " I cannot choose," replies Hotspur :

> Sometimes he angers me,
> With telling me of the moldwarp and the ant,
> Of the dreamer Merlin and his prophecies,
> And of a dragon and a finless fish,
> A clip-wing'd griffin and a moulten raven,
> A couching lion and a ramping cat,
> And such a deal of skimble-skamble stuff,
> As puts me from my faith.

Merlin's prophecies are given at length by Geoffrey of Monmouth, and the allusion to " a finless fish " is a reference to Merlin's prediction that " the lion's whelps shall be transformed to fishes of the sea," which a modern occultist might claim to be a forecast of submarine warfare. But he would doubtless allow that Merlin might have hit on a better simile for an aeroplane than a " clip-wing'd griffin."

The Northumbrian has no patience with mysticism. " He held me," says poor Hotspur—

> Last night at least nine hours
> In reckoning up the several devils' names,
> That were his lackeys . . . O ! he's as tedious
> As is a tired horse, a railing wife. . . .

To Hotspur's denunciation of Glendower's occultism Mortimer makes a reply which may be regarded as Shakespeare's final verdict on the character of Glendower:

> In faith, he is a worthy gentleman,
> Exceedingly well read, and profited
> In strange concealments; valiant as a lion,
> And wondrous affable, and as bountiful as mines in India.

Worcester also remonstrates with Hotspur on his unreasonable attitude.

> My lord [he says], you are too wilful-blame [the text is
>     evidently corrupt].
> You must needs learn, lord, to amend this fault,
> Though sometimes it shows greatness, courage, blood
> (And that's the dearest grace it renders you),
> Yet oftentimes it doth present harsh rage,

> Defect of manners, want of government,
> Pride, haughtiness, opinion and disdain,
> The least of which, haunting a nobleman,
> Loseth men's hearts and leaves behind a stain
> Upon the beauty of all parts besides,
> Beguiling them of commendation.

Upon Glendower's return with the ladies a singular position is disclosed, for as Lady Mortimer greets her husband the latter cries:

> This is the deadly spite that angers me,
> My wife can speak no English, I no Welsh.
> *Glendower.* My daughter weeps: she will not part with you.
> She'll be a soldier too, she'll to the wars.

Which was not mere extravagance on her part. That Welshwomen could be accused of mutilation shows that they followed their fathers, husbands, or sons to battle, doubtless acting as a supply train, just as the Boer women used to accompany their menfolk, acting as carriers, loaders, cooks, nurses, etc.

Mortimer consigns her to the care of her father.

> *Mortimer.* Good father, tell her that she and my aunt Percy
> Shall follow in your conduct speedily.

Glendower, we are told, " speaks to her in Welsh, and she answers him in the same." Then Lady Mortimer, turning to her husband, her eyes bedimmed with tears, attempts to hold converse with

him, but with a pathetic shake of his head Mortimer
replies:

> I understand thy looks: that pretty Welsh,
> Which thou pourest down from these swelling heavens,
> I am too perfect in; and, but for shame,
> In such a parley would I answer thee.
>                         [*She speaks again in Welsh.*
> I understand thy kisses, and thou mine,
> And that's a feeling disputation;
> But I will never be a truant, love,
> Till I have learned thy language; for thy tongue
> Makes Welsh as sweet as ditties highly penned,
> Sung by a fair queen in a summer bower,
> With ravishing division to her lute.

Glendower (who has perhaps interpreted this
speech, thus suggesting to her the idea of song)
explains that his daughter wishes to sing to her
husband before he departs for the war, whereupon
there follows the interesting stage direction: " A
Welsh song sung by Lady Mortimer."

We would give much to know what that Welsh
song was, and whether it was accompanied by
the harp. Brinley Richards, in his *Songs of Wales*,
tells us that many of the old Welsh airs are very
ancient, and with reference to the harp we learn
that there was a revival of that instrument in the
days of Elizabeth. A celebrated Welsh harpist,
Thomas Pritchard (" Twm Bach "), a native of
Glamorganshire, died in London in 1597.

Hotspur and Mortimer depart for the war, and Glendower makes no further appearance upon the stage, but history tells us that he made a triumphant progress through South Wales, besieging Carmarthen Castle, fighting at St. Clears and Laugharne, burning the Bishop's Palace at Llandaff, and capturing Cardiff Castle. Nevertheless, he was absent from Shrewsbury at the crucial moment, " being overruled by the prophecies." And here Shakespeare either purposely or accidentally brings out into strong relief the susceptibility of the Welsh character to the sway of fatalism. Holinshed does not give this explanation of Glendower's absence, so that Shakespeare's allusion to the " prophecies " would seem to be an original touch, unless indeed he had heard some traditional account of the circumstance.

There are many Welsh critics who feel that Shakespeare treated the character of Owain Glyndwr none too kindly by representing him as a mysterious hero who claimed supernatural powers. Shakespeare, however, as we have seen, based his *Henry IV.*, with other plays, on the romantic chronicles of the old uncritical historian Holinshed, who tells of the belief of the people that Glyndwr could " produce storms by art magic." " It may be," says Sir Owen Edwards, " that

Owen Glendower tried to surround himself with mystery. . . . Had he the superstition which is the shadow of fatalism? He consulted a seer when in Merlin's City, now called Carmarthen, and was told he would be taken under a black flag."

Shakespeare was doubtless attracted by Glendower's reputation; for whether he himself was a believer in the supernatural or merely valued it as dramatic material, he has, like other dramatists of the sixteenth century, made extensive use of supernatural incidents, and we have ghosts in *Hamlet, Macbeth, Julius Cæsar,* and *Richard III.,* fairies and elves in *A Midsummer Night's Dream,* spirits and a magician in *The Tempest,* and witches in *Macbeth.* While recognising the value, from the dramatic standpoint, of surrounding Glendower with an atmosphere of mystery, Shakespeare leaves us in no doubt as to his valour, generosity, affability, and erudition.

Owain Glyndwr's proper name was Owen ap Griffith Vaughan. He remained unconquered, for although he was eventually obliged to fall back before the pressure of the English forces, he never abandoned the struggle and was never finally subdued.

The rolls of Parliament and Rymer's *Fœdera* mention that he was excluded from a general amnesty granted by Henry in 1411. In 1412 he was taken prisoner. In 1415, shortly before the Battle of Agincourt, Henry V. commissioned Sir Gilbert Talbot to negotiate with Meredith, Glendower's son, with a view to the pacification of the Welsh leader and his followers. After the victory of Agincourt these overtures were renewed, but to no purpose; Glendower " resolved to live and die free, a prince without subjects or country, rather than the subject of the conqueror of Wales. He still continued to haunt the wilds and mountains of Snowdon, and, if we may believe one tradition, died peaceably at his daughter's house at Mornington in 1415, while another shows us his burial-place beneath the great window of the south aisle of Bangor Cathedral. Both accounts can very well be true, but wherever Owen Glendower rests there rests the dust of a man who only wanted a wider field and a more numerous people to have become the saviour as he was the true hero of his country."[*]

Tradition tells us of an incident with the relation of which we may fittingly close this chapter. Early one morning, while the Abbot of Valle Crucis was praying on the hillside near the abbey, Owain Glyndwr appeared and said, " Sir Abbot, you have risen too early." " No," said the Abbot, " it is you have risen too early by a hundred years."

[*] Cassell's *History of England.*

# CHAPTER X

## SIR HUGH EVANS

TRADITION has it that Queen Elizabeth, delighted by the escapades of Falstaff in *King Henry IV.*, expressed a wish to see the fat knight as lover; whereupon Shakespeare straightway set to work upon the comedy of the *Merry Wives of Windsor*, completing the play within a fortnight. The character which concerns us in this comedy is of course that of Sir Hugh Evans, who is described in the *dramatis personnæ* as " a Welsh parson." He was a schoolmaster-parson, just as Thomas Jenkins might have been at Stratford-upon-Avon, for we are told that the headmaster of the Stratford Grammar School acted as chaplain of the Guild chapel adjoining. For a time, indeed, the school was held in the chapel itself. That Shakespeare had Thomas Jenkins in mind when he created the character of Sir Hugh Evans appears more than probable when we remember that the "Welsh parson " is introduced in the company of two Warwickshire worthies, Mr. Justice Shallow and Slender, his cousin, of whom the former is an

undoubted caricature of Sir Thomas Lucy of Charlecote Park.

It is "Sir Hugh's highest ambition to be the
oracle of the town in which he is schoolmaster.
He is fond of popularity; and will readily do little
kindnesses for his friends, negotiate marriages for
their daughters, and settle their differences when
they threaten to be serious; and is nothing loath
to enjoy a good dinner at some kind neighbour's
expense. We laugh with Sir Hugh rather than
at him. There is a vein of shrewdness in Sir Hugh
which prevents him from being ridiculous. It is
the shrewdness of a Welshman, and it is in precisely
the accurate conception of this point that the
merit of the dramatist lies " (Newell).

We learn at the very outset that Sir Hugh is a
man of peace. " If Sir John Falstaff have committed disparagements unto you," he tells Mr.
Justice Shallow, " I am of the church, and will be
glad to do my benevolence to make atonements
and compromises between you." He is a man of
" goot discretions," a serious man, impatient of
" pribbles and prabbles." His strong regard for
the truth is shown by his emphatic, if somewhat
tautological declaration, " I do despise a liar as I
do despise one who is false, or as I do despise one
who is not true." He bids his friends walk in the

143

straight path so that they may not suffer " for a pad conscience." They should also " pray " and not follow " the imaginations of their own hearts." He is a methodical man; if they entrust him with a mission he will " make a prief of it " on his note-book and " afterwards 'ork upon the cause with as great discreetly as we can." He is a man of common sense; Pistol's heroics he dismisses as " affectations." When he declares he is only pre-pared to " description the matter " if his auditor " be capacity of it " we seem to catch a glimpse of his schoolmaster model. He loves in his pedantic fashion to be exact. " Let us command to know that of your mouth or your lips," he observes, " for divers philosophers hold that the lips is parcel of the mouth." We get a glimpse of his fondness for good living when, in despatching Simple with a message, he bids him begone, as he " wants to make an end of his dinner," particularly as " there is pippins and cheese to come." Cheese, by the way, presumably in the form of Welsh rarebits, or roasted with pippins, appears to be a weakness of his, for we find Ford exclaiming, " I will rather trust Parson Hugh the Welshman with my cheese than my wife with herself."

Attempting to forward the suit of his friend Slender for the hand of Ann Page, he involves

144

himself in a quarrel which results in a challenge from the fiery Dr. Caius, the French physician, who is Slender's rival.

" By Gar," exclaims the Doctor in his frenzy, "I will cut his troat in the Park. I will teach the jack-a-nape Priest to meddle or make." But Sir Hugh, though a man of peace, is not a man of "peace at any price"; sinking the parson in the Celt, he accepts the challenge, and mine host of the Garter is commissioned to make arrangements for the duel. Mine host, being of a waggish disposition, plays a practical joke upon the intending combatants, arranging that they shall await each other in different fields, with the result that each believes that the other has shirked the encounter.

In a field near Windsor the Frenchman impatiently awaits the coming of the " Jack Priest," and commenting upon his absence to his serving-man, Jack Rugby, he exclaims: "By gar, he is save his soul that he is no come. He has pray his Pible vell dat he is no come; by gar, Jack Rugby, he is dead already if he be come."

" He is wise, Sir," says Jack Rugby; "he knew your worship would kill him if he came."

" By gar," continues the irate Frenchman, " de herring is no dead so as I vill kill him."

At this point there enters the Host, Shallow,

Slender, and Page, to whom Caius explains that the "coward Jack Priest of the vorld" has not dared to show his face. "I pray you bear vitness," he adds, "that me have stay six or seven, two, tree hours for him and he is no come."

In a field at Frogmore Sir Hugh Evans and "good master Slender's serving man and friend Simple, by your name" (and also by nature) is awaiting the coming of the French physician. Sir Hugh discloses the turbulence of his feelings by the words, "Pless my soul, how full of cholers I am, and trempling of mind!" At one moment he sings to keep up his courage, at another moment he has "a great dispositions to cry."

While he is in this anxious frame of mind Page, Shallow, and Slender appear upon the scene. They affect surprise at the spectacle of the schoolmaster-parson abroad in the fields with sword and doublet and hose on "such a raw rheumatic day."

Sir Hugh explains mysteriously that "there is reasons and causes for it," but when it is mentioned that in another field the renowned French physician is awaiting some person from whom he has suffered wrong, Sir Hugh loses his temper for the first time.

"Got's will and his passion of my heart," he exclaims, "I had as lief you would tell me of a mess

of porridge. He has no more knowledge of Hibbo-
crates and Galen—and he is a knave besides, a
cowardly knave, as you would desires to be acquainted withal."

But here the Host and Doctor Caius arrive,
and mine Host, having advised the "soul curer
and body curer" to put up their swords and to
" hack our English"instead of their limbs, confesses
the trick which he has played upon them; and
in the end the spectators depart in high feather
to celebrate the humour of the situation at the
Garter.

Caius, the true position dawning upon him,
shakes his fist in impotent wrath after the retreat-
ing company. "Ha! do I perceive dat? Have
you make-a de sot of us? Ha, ha!" he ejaculates.

And the erstwhile enemies become companions
in wrathful resentment. "He has made us his
vlouting-stog [laughing-stock]," says Evans. "I
desire you that we may be friends, and let us knog
our brains together, to be revenge on this same
scaull, scurvy, cogging companion, the host of the
Garter."

"By gar, vit all my heart," responds Caius;
" he promise to bring me vere is Anne Page; by
gar, he deceive me too."

"Well," replies Sir Hugh, with a fierceness not

wholly assumed, for he is still incensed, " I will smite his noddles,—Pray you, follow."

Caius and Evans have not long to wait for their revenge. And thereby hangs a tale: a curious fragment of unimportant history. In the year 1593 the Duke of Würtemberg visited England, travelling the roads—perhaps because he was unwilling, for economic reasons, to bring with him a retinue commensurate with his majesty—under the name of Count Mompelgard. He remained a month in this country, visiting the Queen; from August 17th to 19th he was at Reading, and from there proceeded to Windsor; and he also halted at, or passed through, Maidenhead and Colnbrook. As a royal visitor to the Court he was granted the right to requisition post-horses free of charge. Like a true German, he made the most liberal use of his privilege, and no official compensation was forthcoming. He was a pompous person who exacted much deference; in short, he did not make himself beloved. The victims, of course, were loud in their complaints; the story of the German " cousin " of the Queen ran the rounds of the posting-houses, and must have been a matter of gossip in the London taverns.

Bearing these facts in mind, we are able to appreciate the humour of Act IV., Scene 3, and the constant play on the word " cousin " on which Evans wittily and maliciously rings the changes. Bardolph informs the Host that he will be required to furnish horses. " Sir, the Germans desire to have three of your horses: the duke himself will be to-morrow at court, and they are going to meet him."

" What duke should that be comes so secretly?" says the Host. " I hear not of him in the court. Let me speak with the gentlemen: they speak English? . . . They shall have my horses, but I'll make them pay. . . . They have had my house a week at command; I have turned away my other guests." From which it would seem that the German " gentlemen " had insisted upon having the inn kept empty, either because the duke was expected, or because they chose to pretend that he was expected. The horses are supplied; Bardolph evidently makes one of the party, presumably because he is to bring the horses back. He returns in Act IV., Scene 5.

*Bardolph*. Out, alas, sir! cozenage, mere cozenage!

*Host*. Where be my horses? speak well of them, varletto.

*Bardolph*. Run away with the cozeners; for so soon as I came beyond Eton, they threw me off from behind one of them in a slough of mire, and set spurs, and away, like three German devils, three Doctor Faustuses.

*Host*. They are gone but to meet the duke, villain: do not say they be fled; Germans are honest men.

The revenge sought by the Welsh parson and the French doctor takes the form of a solemn admonition to lock the stable door after the horses are stolen.

We may imagine them to have seen the sorry and miry Bardolph limping back from Eton; to have questioned him, or to have heard his tale from the sympathetic townsfolk to whom he no doubt related it as he neared the Garter. Bubbling over with malicious glee, Evans gravely enters the inn. " Where is mine host ?" he says. " Have a care of your entertainments : there is a friend of mine come to town, tells me there is three cousin*-Germans, that has cozened all the hosts of Reading, of Maidenhead, of Colnbrook, of horses and money. I tell you for good-will, look you ; you are wise, and full of gibes and vlouting-stogs, and it is not convenient you should be cozened. Fare you well." And no sooner has he gone than Doctor Caius looks in to give the same warning, but whereas Sir Hugh Evans has sufficient self-restraint to leave his ready wit unhampered, Doctor Caius is brimming over with exuberant malice, and blurts out his news

* It is probable that the document furnished in the Queen's name, to be shown to keepers of posting-houses, etc., began somewhat as follows : " Whereas," or " know by these presents our *cousin,*" etc., and that the wording of it had become public property.

in a downright manner, forgetting what little
English syntax he knows in his excitement.

*Caius.* Vere is mine host de Jartiere ?
*Host.* Here, master doctor, in perplexity, and doubtful
dilemma.
*Caius.* I cannot tell vat is dat; but it is tell-a me, dat you
make grand preparation for a duke de Jarmany: by my trot,
dere is no duke dat de court is know to come. I tell you for
good vill ! adieu !

Mine Host is a man of substance, but the loss
of three horses is no trifle. Fenton, full of his
projected elopement with Anne Page, finds him
in the dumps; for once his readiness to take part
in any frolic or piece of mischief or adventure has
deserted him. " Master Fenton, talk not to me:
my mind is heavy; I will give over all." But
Fenton is not to be put off with this.

*Fenton.* Yet hear me speak. Assist me in my purpose,
And, as I am a gentleman, I'll give thee
A hundred pound in gold more than your loss.

At which comfortable assurance the Host takes
heart and consents to listen, and, finally, to " procure the vicar " for the runaway match.

It is interesting to note that the words " Germans
are honest men " are not in the Quarto. The
statement is not a serious expression of opinion;
mine Host is only seeking to comfort himself.
Such as it is, it may have been absent from the

original version, for it certainly was not Shakespeare's opinion. What he personally thought of the Germans is reflected in the following passage from *The Merchant of Venice*, Act I., Scene 2 :

> *Nerissa.* How like you the young German, the Duke of Saxony's nephew ?
> *Portia.* Very vilely in the morning, when he is sober, and most vilely in the afternoon, when he is drunk; when he is best he is a little worse than a man; and when he is worst, he is little better than a beast: an the worst fall that ever fell I shall make shift to go without him. . . . I will do anything, Nerissa, ere I will be married to a sponge.

The Count of Palatine, presumably another German, is " full of unmannerly sadness," with " a bad habit of frowning."

In Act IV., Scene 8 of the third part of *King Henry VI.* Shakespeare speaks of the " hasty Germans." Complaints of articles " made in Germany " were heard long before our time. Biron, in Act III., Scene 1 of *Love's Labour's Lost*, compares a woman to—

> A German clock
> Still a-repairing; ever out of frame,
> And never going aright, being a watch,
> But being watched that it may still go right.

In *Much Ado About Nothing* Shakespeare describes a German as being " from the waist down all slops " (the slops referring to their nether garments), and in *Cymbeline*, (Act II. Scene 5) we have, " Like a full-acorned boar, a German one."

When Falstaff goes through his last ordeal as " Herne the Hunter " (which brings us once again into contact with Welsh mythology), Evans, disguised as a Satyr, calls his fairies into a ring.

> Pray you, lock hand in hand: yourselves in order set,
> And twenty glow-worms shall our lanterns be
> To guide our measure round about the tree.
> But stay ! I smell a man of middle earth !

There is evidently something in that " pray you," and in the accent of the satyr, which falls familiarly upon the fat knight's ear, for he whispers a heartfelt prayer: " Heaven defend me from that Welch fairy, lest he transform me to a piece of cheese."

" The Welsh parson," says Hazlitt, " is an excellent character in all respects. He is as respectable as he is humorous." H. C. Hart endorses this view, and adds: " Like all Shakespeare's schoolmasters, Sir Hugh Evans is at once simple and pedantic. In the duelling scene he is capital. We are indebted to Sir Hugh Evans for a number of interesting allusions. It is satisfactory to find him in an honourable position at the close, not in the ignominious situation occupied by Caius and Slender."

Hunter has the following interesting comments on the characters of the Welsh parson and the French physician:

" Sir Hugh Evans, who is the representative of the curate and pedagogue conjoined of the time, speaks in his broad Welsh accent. This kind of speech must have been very familiar to Shakespeare in his youth, so many Welsh people having taken up their abode at Stratford; and that this early familiarity with the Welsh mode of pronouncing the English language had something to do with the origination of the characters of Sir Hugh and of Fluellen appears from this, that we have no exhibition of the peculiar pronunciation of either Scottish or Irish persons in any of the plays, or of the peculiar dialect of any particular district in England. The question raised by Dr. Johnson whether Shakespeare was ' the first writer to produce upon the English stage the effect of language distorted and depraved by provincial or foreign pronunciation ' has been set at rest, and Shakespeare was certainly not the first; but he was perhaps the first who introduced Welsh. . . . As in Sir Hugh we have the Welsh pronunciation, so in Dr. Caius we have the broken English of a Frenchman. His broken English and his irascible temper are his *raisons d'être ;* he is crudely painted as compared with Evans, and we have no idea what sort of a physician he may have been. He is an amusing character, but the poet has been unfortunate in the choice of a name. There was a real Dr. Caius, an Englishman, whose hereditary name of Kaye was thus Latinised and has been lost in this more scholastic form, who lived so near the poet's time that his name had not passed out of the popular mind, while it was reverenced amongst scholars for his noble foundation at Cambridge. The memory of this admirable person was in danger of being defamed by the supposition that he was the person indicated by the Dr. Caius of this play; and it is to be feared that there are persons still in whose minds the real and the dramatic Dr. Caius are confounded. The Dr. Caius of Shakespeare is a representative of a class of persons who are held in little esteem by the native practitioners of the art of medicine—foreigners who introduced nostrums or had perhaps attained in foreign Universities a skill beyond that of the English physicians. . . . There is one point in connection with Dr. Caius and the Welsh curate which I cannot forbear mentioning, although it is very improbable that it was known to Shakespeare when he made Dr. Caius utter so many contemptuous expressions respecting his Welsh antagonist.

The point is this: that the real Dr. Caius in the statutes of the College founded by him specially excludes persons who are Welshmen from holding any of his fellowships."

Hunter's authority for this latter statement is the *Cambridge Portfolio* for 1839.

It may be noted that Dr. Caius died in 1573, four or five years before the reputed date of the *Merry Wives*. He was born at Norwich, but travelled and studied on the Continent. Like Shakespeare's doctor, he was a physician at the Court (of King Edward VI. and Queen Mary).

Fleay has a theory which would, if well founded, dispose of our suggestion that Thomas Jenkins was the prototype of Evans. It appears, however, to be the merest conjecture. " I believe," he says, " that in Shakespeare's play Evans and Dr. Caius are satirical representations of Drayton and Lodge. Drayton is introduced as Evan, a Welsh attorney, by Jonson in *For the Honour of Wales*, and Lodge was frequently satirised on the stage as a French doctor."

The expression put into the mouth of Parson Evans (Act III., Scene 1), " I had as lief you would tell me of a mess of porridge," has been cited by the Rev. Thomas Carter as one of the proofs that the Bible which Shakespeare used was the Geneva

version. " Parson Evans seems to have on his mind
the knavery by which Jacob tricked Esau his
brother," says Mr. Carter, though it is more reason-
able to suggest that the phrase was familiar to
Shakespeare; and " mess of porridge " would
seem to be a misquotation for " mess of pottage."
Curiously enough, these words do not occur in the
Bible narrative itself, but appear in the chapter-
heading of Gen. xxv. in the Geneva version:
" Esau selleth his birthright for a messe of pottage."
The heading does not occur in the Authorised
Version."

# CHAPTER XI

## KING HENRY V.—"HARRY OF MONMOUTH"

HENRY V. was born at Monmouth Castle, and Monmouthshire, before the Act of Union of England and Wales (passed in the reign of Henry VIII.), was a Welsh county. It was no doubt this circumstance which caused Shakespeare to represent the King as being of Welsh descent. He was not a Welshman by race. He was descended from Edward III., through John of Gaunt, by his first wife Blanche, daughter of Henry Duke of Lancaster. His father was Henry IV., his mother Mary Bohun. It is necessary, for the sake of accuracy, that this should be mentioned; but what concerns us here is that Shakespeare regards him as a Welshman, and makes him announce himself as such when challenged by Pistol. It is worthy of note that, while the King as Prince Hal was sowing his wild oats, nothing was said as to his Welsh nationality, though, had the dramatist any fault to find with the Welsh, here was his opportunity. It was only when—

Consideration like an angel came
And whipped the offending Adam out of him,

that any mention was made of the Welsh blood in his veins.

When Henry ascended the throne his wildness had " mortified " in him. All his dissipated associates had been discarded, the roystering Falstaff had for his own good been banished from the temptations of London, and the reformed monarch took into his favour a more worthy and more suitable follower in the person of the loyal, brave, and high-spirited Fluellen.

There are many allusions in the play of *King Henry V.* which are of interest to a Welsh reader, and it is as a Welshman that King Henry speaks when he delivers his famous address to his troops before Harfleur.

> *K. Hen.* Once more unto the breach, dear friends, once
>   more:
> Or close the wall up with our English dead !
> In peace, there's nothing so becomes a man,
> As modest stillness and humility:
> But when the blast of war blows in our ears,
> Then imitate the action of the tiger;
> Stiffen the sinews, summon up the blood,
> Disguise fair nature with hard-favour'd rage,
> Then lend the eye a terrible aspect;
> Let it pry through the portage* of the head,
> Like the brass cannon; let the brow o'erwhelm it,†
> As fearfully as doth a galled‡ rock

---

* The eye-sockets.　† O'erhang.　‡ Worn by the waves.

O'erhang and jutty* his confounded base
Swill'd with the wild and wasteful ocean.
Now set the teeth, and stretch the nostril wide;
Hold hard the breath, and bend up every spirit
To his full height!—On, on, you noblest English,
Whose blood is fet† from fathers of war-proof!
Fathers, that, like so many Alexanders,
Have, in these parts, from morn till even fought,
And sheathed their swords for lack of argument.‡
Dishonour not your mothers: now attest,
That those, whom you called fathers did beget you!
Be copy now to men of grosser blood,
And teach them how to war!—and you, good yeomen,
Whose limbs were made in England, show us here
The mettle of your pasture; let us swear
That you are worth your breeding, which I doubt not
For there is none of you so mean and base,
That hath not noble lustre in your eyes.
I see you stand like greyhounds in the slips,
Straining upon the start. The game's afoot:
Follow your spirit, and upon this charge
Cry "God for Harry, England, and Saint George!"
[*Exeunt. Alarum, and chambers go off.*

In Act. IV., Scene 7, when Fluellen, speaking of the leek and how it came to be the Welsh national emblem, says, "I do believe your majesty takes no scorn to wear the leek upon Saint Tavy's day," whereupon King Henry answers:

I wear it for a memorable honour;
For I am Welsh, you know, good countryman.
*Fluellen.* All the water in Wye cannot wash your majesty's

---

\* Project beyond.          † Fetched.
‡ *I.e.*, having placed all their adversaries *hors de combat.*

Welsh plood out of your pody, I can tell you that; Got pless it and preserve it, as long as it pleases his grace, and his majesty too ! . . . By Jeshu, I am your majesty's country-man, I care not who know it. . . .

Did Shakespeare fear that his humorous exploitation of the Welshman's English might be taken amiss by Welshmen, or even by the Queen, who was of Welsh descent? If so, he makes amends in Act V., Scene 1, when Gower, rebuking the discomfited Pistol, says:

I have seen you gleeking and galling at this gentleman twice or thrice. You thought, because he could not speak English in the native garb, he could not handle au English cudgel. . . . Henceforth let a Welsh correction teach you a good English condition.

## CHAPTER XII

### FLUELLEN

FLUELLEN is the type of the brave, patriotic, honourable, loyal, high-spirited Welshman. Shakespeare evidently intended him to be a favourite with his audience, for we see more of him, perhaps, than of any non-essential character in *King Henry V.*, and he is depicted as being on terms of easy familiarity with the King.

" Among his thousand characters," says Froude, " there is not one which Shakespeare has sketched more tenderly or with a more loving and affectionate irony." Fluellen is the most prominent figure of an interesting group of captains—Welsh, Scotch, and Irish—which the poet may well have introduced in order to promote the cause of national unity by representing the four nations of the kingdom as sharing in the glories of a campaign which had for its triumphant termination the immortal victory of Agincourt. It is true that relations between the four representatives are not always perfectly harmonious, but, whatever their personal differences, they are agreed to fight under

the same flag. King Henry expresses his apprecia-
tion of the Welshman when he says:

> For I do know Fluellen, valiant,
> And touched with choler, hot as gunpowder,
> And quickly will return an injury.

He is recognised as an authority on ticklish
points of honour; the King himself is glad to consult
him as an authority on such matters. Defending
his honour to a private soldier, who does not recog-
nise him, he wears the man's glove as a gage, giving
the man a glove of his own, the understanding
being that they will settle their quarrel after the
battle. Fluellen is appealed to: is the soldier to
keep his word, no matter what the quality of his
opponent?

*King Henry.* What think you, Captain Fluellen : is it fit
this soldier keep his oath?
*Fluellen.* He is a craven and a villain else, an't please your
majesty, in my conscience.
*King Henry.* It may be his enemy is a gentleman of great
sort, quite from the answer of his degree.
*Fluellen.* Though he be as good a gentleman as the devil is,
as Lucifer and Belzebub himself, it is necessary, look your
grace, that he keep his vow, and his oath: if he be perjured,
see you now, his reputation is as arrant a villain and a
Jack-sauce as ever his black shoe trod upon God's ground and
his earth, in his conscience, la.

It has been suggested that Sir David Gam was
the prototype of Fluellen, but there seems to be

163

little warrant for this assumption. Sir David
Gam is mentioned only in the list of the " English
dead." If Shakespeare had had the Brecon Welshman in his mind in creating the character of
Fluellen he would hardly have omitted some
reference to the tradition that credits the Welsh
Knight with having been instrumental in saving
the King's life. Moreover, we may confidently
assume that Sir David Gam's quaint report on the
force and position of the enemy, " There is enough
to be killed, enough to be taken, and enough to
run away," would have formed a subject of comment
by the King, and the heroic end of Gam and his
companions would hardly have been omitted.*

If the character was sketched from life, Shakespeare's model was more probably Sir Roger
Williams, an intrepid Welshman and soldier of
fortune, who fought in the armies of Queen Elizabeth and Henry of Navarre. A writer in the

* Eighteen French knights banded themselves together
to kill the English King. Gam, with two companions, frus-
trated the attempt. Tradition says that the three heroes
accounted for fourteen of the enemy, but were themselves slain.
If Shakespeare had this incident in mind it may account for
Henry's suspicion when he sees a party of horsemen on a hill
in Act IV., Scene 7. But in Act IV., Scene 8, when Henry is
given a list of the dead, he reads " Davy Gam, esquire," without
comment, which seems to argue that the incident had escaped
the poet.

*Welsh Outlook* for March, 1915 (Chapter IV.) tells us that " a few years before Shakespeare wrote his *King Henry V.* there had died in London a Welshman whose name was a household word to every member of the theatre, and whose character presents some very remarkable similarities to that of Fluellen. Sir Roger Williams was one of the most daring and picturesque knights of the sword that even that country which has produced an Owen Lawgoch and a Picton can boast of. . . . He was born at Penrhos in Monmouthshire, and in this connection it is impossible not to recall Fluellen's eulogy of the Wye, and the terms of his admiration for King Henry."

Like Fluellen, Sir Roger Williams " was of an impulsive, choleric, courageous nature," but yet as ready as that lovable champion of the leek to end his many quarrels and duels amicably.

Fluellen is a great stickler for the " rules and disciplines of the war," and Captain Gower is his boon companion, because he is " literatured in the wars." The Welsh captain refuses to yield, in his knowledge of the proper methods of warfare, even to the Duke of Gloucester himself. " Tell you the Duke," he observes to Captain Gower, who has brought a message from Gloucester, " it is not good to come to the mines, for, look you, the mines is not according to the disciplines of the war."

When Captain Gower mentions that the Duke, to whom the order of the siege has been given, is altogether directed by Captain Macmorris, we learn that Fluellen has no great opinion of the Irish captain; after close observation the Welshman has come to the conclusion that " he is an ass, as in the world . . . he has no more directions in the true disciplines of the wars, look you, of the Roman disciplines, than is a puppy-dog."*

Of Captain Jamy, the Scotsman, he has a very much better opinion, for the Scotsman, " a marvellous falorous gentleman," can " maintain his argument as any military man in the world, in the disciplines of the pristine wars of the Romans."

The Scotsman exhibits all the national love of dialectics, but is as willing to listen to the arguments of others. " I wad full fain heard some question between you tway," he tells Fluellen and Macmorris. The Irishman, although a courageous soldier, is touchy and impatient of argument, making the excuse that " the day is hot, and the weather, and the wars, and the king, and the duke," and " the town is beseeched," and " the trumpet calls." Captain Jamy declares that he intends to do his

* This is the only Irish character created by Shakespeare.

duty before he sleeps, " ay, or go to death "; but he would be glad to hear a debate between the Welshman and the Irishman. Thus encouraged, Fluellen proceeds, addressing Captain Macmorris: " I think, look you, under correction, there is not many of your nation——" But the peppery Macmorris sees a covert insult in this reference to his nation, and declares that the man who talks of his nation is " a villain, and a bastard, and a knave, and a rascal."

Fluellen becomes dangerously polite. " Look you," he says, " if you take the matter otherwise than is meant, Captain Macmorris, peradventure I shall think you do not use me with that affability as in discretion you ought to use me, look you, being as good a man as yourself, both in the disciplines of wars, and in the derivation of my birth, and in other particulars." Macmorris denies that Fluellen is as good a man as himself, " so Crish save me, I will cut off your head "; but the trumpet sounds in time to break off the quarrel.

Later in the play are passages between the swaggering Pistol and Fluellen. Pistol, knowing that Fluellen is in favour with the Duke of Exeter, beseeches him to intervene on behalf of Bardolph, who has stolen a pyx out of a church, and is condemned to be hanged as a discouragement to looters; but Fluellen's respect for discipline is proof against all personal blandishments, and he declares definitely and emphatically that " if he were his brother " he would not under the circumstances ask for his reprieve, " for discipline ought to be used."

Pistol's ire is aroused, and he expresses a hope that Fluellen may " die and be damn'd." This insult is not lost on Fluellen, for, turning to Captain Gower, who is a spectator of the scene, he observes significantly: " It is very well; what he has spoke to me, that is well, I warrant you, when time is serve."

How the time served we learn in Act V., Scene 1.

King Henry, while proceeding on a tour of inspection incognito, shows his friendship for Fluellen in an interesting passage with Pistol.

> *Pistol.* What is thy name ?
> *K. Hen.* Harry le Roy.
> *Pist.* Le Roy ! a Cornish name: art thou of Cornish crew ?
> *K. Hen.* No, I am a Welshman.
> *Pist.* Know'st thou Fluellen ?
> *K. Hen.* Yes.
> *Pist.* Tell him, I'll knock his leek about his pate
> Upon Saint Davy's day.
> *K. Hen.* Do not you wear your dagger in your cap that day, lest he knock that about yours.
> *Pist.* Art thou his friend ?
> *K. Hen.* And his kinsman too.

*Pist.* The figo for thee, then !
*K. Hen.* I thank you : God be with you !
*Pist.* My name is Pistol call'd. [*Exit.*
*K. Hen.* It sorts well with your fierceness.

Immediately following upon this Fluellen and Gower appear upon the scene, and the King, hearing Fluellen's admonition to Gower to " speak lower " in the presence of the enemy, exclaims, in an admiring aside:

> Though it appear a little out of fashion,
> There is much care and valour in this Welshman.

If there is one virtue more than another that Fluellen possesses it is his intense loyalty to his King. His admiration for Henry is indeed so great that he does not hesitate to compare him with the most famous military leader in the history of the world. This ingenious comparison occurs in a conversation between Fluellen and Gower. King Henry was born at Monmouth, says the admiring Fluellen; " Alexander the Pig " was born in Macedon. If Captain Gower will only look at the maps of the world he will find the situations, " look you," both alike. There is a river in Macedon, and " there is also, moreover, a river at Monmouth." The river at Monmouth is called the Wye, but Fluellen has forgotten the name of the Macedonian river. However, that is of no importance; the point is that they are both alike, and "there is salmons in both." Moreover, while Alexander, "being a little intoxicates in his prains, did, in his ales and his angers, look you, kill his pest friend, Cleitus . . . so Harry Monmouth, being in his right wits and his good judgments, turned away the fat knight with the great belly-doublet "— namely, Falstaff. "I tell you," he concludes triumphantly, "there is goot men porn at Monmouth."

In the dramatic scene before Agincourt, when the King learns that the French have been defeated, the patriotic Fluellen remembers the services of the Welsh in a previous battle, and at the same time explains the origin of the leek as a national emblem.

*Montjoy.*          The day is yours.
*K. Hen.* Praised be God, and not our strength, for it!
What is this castle call'd that stands hard by?
*Mont.* They call it Agincourt.
*K. Hen.* Then call we this the field of Agincourt,
Fought on the day of Crispin Crispianus.
*Flu.* Your grandfather of famous memory, an't please your majesty, and your great-uncle Edward the Plack Prince of Wales, as I have read in the chronicles, fought a most prave pattle here in France.
*K. Hen.* They did, Fluellen.
*Flu.* Your majesty says very true: if your majesties is remembered of it, the Welshmen did good service in a garden where leeks did grow, wearing leeks in their Monmouth caps;

which, your majesty know, to this hour is an honourable
badge of the service; and I do believe your majesty takes no
scorn to wear the leek upon Saint Tavy's day.

*K. Hen.* I wear it for a memorable honour;
For I am Welsh, you know, good countryman.

*Flu.* All the water in Wye cannot wash your majesty's
Welsh plood out of your pody, I can tell you that: God pless
it and preserve it, as long as it pleases his grace, and his
majesty too !

*K. Hen.* Thanks, good my countryman.

*Flu.* By Jeshu, I am your majesty's countryman, I care
not who know it; I will confess it to all the 'orld: I need not
to be ashamed of your majesty, praised be God, so long as
your majesty is an honest man.

*K. Hen.* God keep me so !

In the incident of the glove Fluellen again shows
his loyalty to his King, but he does not rise to the
full height of his greatness until we come to the
scene in Act V. in which he vindicates the honour
of his native land by making Pistol devour the leek
which he had so frequently disparaged.  The scene
is an English camp in France.

*Enter* FLUELLEN *and* GOWER.

*Gow.* Nay, that's right; but why wear you your leek to-day?
Saint Davy's day is past.

*Flu.* There is occasions and causes why and wherefore in
all things: I will tell you, asse my friend, Captain Gower:
the rascally, scauld, beggarly, pragging knave, Pistol, which
you and yourself and all the world know to be no petter than
a fellow, look you now, of no merits, he is come to me and
prings me pread and salt yesterday, look you, and bid me eat
my leek: it ¡was in a place where I could not breed no con-

tention with him; but I will be so bold as to wear it in my cap till I see him once again, and then I will tell him a little piece of my desires.

*Enter* PISTOL.

*Gow.* Why, here he comes, swelling like a turkey-cock.

*Flu.* 'Tis no matter for his swellings nor his turkey-cocks. God pless you, Aunchient* Pistol! you scurvy knave, God pless you!

*Pist.* Ha! art thou Bedlam? dost thou thirst, base Trojan, To have me fold up Parca's fatal web?†
Hence! I am qualmish at the smell of leek.

*Flu.* I peseech you heartily, scurvy knave, at my desires, and my requests, and my petitions, to eat, look you, this leek: because, look you, you do not love it, nor your affections and your appetites and your disgestions doo's not agree with it, I would desire you to eat it.

*Pist.* Not for Cadwallader and all his goats.

*Flu.* There is one goat for you. [*Strikes him.*] Will you be so good, scauld knave, as eat it?

*Pist.* Base Trojan, thou shalt die.‡

*Flu.* You say very true, scauld knave, when God's will is: I will desire you to live in the mean time, and eat your victuals: come, there is sauce for it. [*Strikes him.*] You called me yesterday mountain-squire; but I will make you to-day a squire of low degree. I pray you, fall to: if you can mock a leek, you can eat a leek. . . . Bite, I pray you; it is good for your green wound and your ploody coxcomb.

*Pist.* Must I bite?

*Flu.* Yes, certainly, and out of doubt and out of question too, and ambiguities.

---

* Ancient = ensign.  See *Othello*.

† The three fates were called *Parcæ* in Latin.  The one who cut through the web of man's life was known as *Atropos*.

‡ According to Geoffrey of Monmouth, the Trojans were the progenitors of the Welsh.  This explanation seems to have been missed by most commentators.

*Pist.* By this leek, I will most horribly revenge:
I, eat and eat ? I swear—
*Flu.* Eat, I pray you: will you have some more sauce to your leek ? there is not enough leek to swear by. . . . Nay, pray you, throw none away; the skin is good for your broken coxcomb. When you take occasions to see leeks hereafter, I pray you, mock at 'em; that is all.

Was Shakespeare, who evidently liked the Welsh, annoyed by the manner in which the London populace jeered at the savoury emblem ? Did he wish to read the " groundlings " a lesson ? It is conceivable; why else, in an historical play, does he stop the action for some six or eight minutes while Fuellen teaches Pistol to respect the national vegetable ? And why else should Captain Gower point the moral in such definite terms ?

*Pist.* All hell shall stir for this.
*Gow.* Go, go; you are a counterfeit cowardly knave. Will you mock at an ancient tradition, begun upon an honourable respect, and worn as a memorable trophy of predeceased valour and dare not avouch in your deeds any of your words ? I have seen you gleeking and galling at this gentleman twice or thrice. You thought, because he could not speak English in the native garb, he could not therefore handle an English cudgel: you find it otherwise; and henceforth let a Welsh correction teach you a good English condition. Fare ye well.                                        [*Exit.*

We have seen elsewhere what various explanations have been given of the wearing of the leek. Dr. Owen Pughe suggests that it arose from the practice of each farmer contributing his leek to the common repast when they met at the Cymmortha, an association by which they gave one another mutual assistance in ploughing the land.

The wearing of the leek appears to have become a royal custom. In 1695 we read how William II. wore a leek on St. David's Day " presented to him by Sergeant Porter, who hath as perquisites all the wearing apparel his majestie had on that day even to his sword."

Fluellen's confident bearing and outspokenness in the presence of the King might seem strange to an Englishman unacquainted with Welsh characteristics; but Shakespeare had evidently noticed a trait to which Giraldus Cambrensis calls attention in his twelfth-century *Description of Wales*, that " Nature hath given not only to the highest, but also to the inferior classes of the people of this nation, a boldness and confidence in speaking and answering, even in the presence of their princes and chieftains." (Book I., c. xv.)

# CHAPTER XIII

## HENRY VII. (THE FIRST TUDOR MONARCH)

THE list of the *dramatis personæ* of the third part of *King Henry VI.* includes the name of " Henry, Earl of Richmond, a youth." In Act IV., Scene 6, there is a gathering in a room in the Tower. The King has just proposed to make Warwick and Clarence protectors of his kingdom, since he wishes to lead a retired life, " and in devotion spend his latter days," when his gaze falls upon Richmond, and the following colloquy takes place between the monarch and the Duke of Somerset:

*King Henry.* My Lord of Somerset, what youth is that,
Of whom you seem to have so tender care ?
*Somerset.* My liege, it is young Henry, Earl of Richmond.
*King Henry.* Come hither, England's hope. [*Lays his hand on his head.*] If secret powers
Suggest but truth to my divining thoughts,
This pretty lad will prove our country's bliss.
His looks are full of peaceful majesty,
His head by nature fram'd to wear a crown,
His hand to wield a sceptre, and himself
Likely, in time, to bless a regal throne.
Make much of him, my lords, for this is he,
Must help you more than you are hurt by me.

It is interesting to compare this passage with one in Bacon's *History of King Henry VII.* " One day," says Bacon, " when King Henry VI., whose innocence gave him holiness, was washing his hands at a great feast, he cast his eyes upon Henry VII., then a young youth, and said, ' This is the lad that shall possess quietly that we now strive for.' "

The subject of this prophecy was the son of Edmund Tudor and Margaret Beaufort, the great-grand-daughter of John of Gaunt by his third wife Catherine Swynford. Richmond was thus descended, on his father's side, from the Welsh gentleman Owen Tudor, and on his mother's side from Edward III. How the royal prophecy was fulfilled becomes apparent during the progress of the play of *King Richard III.*

Henry was born at Pembroke Castle in 1456. His father died shortly before his birth, and he was placed in the care of his uncle, Jasper Tudor. His early years were spent in the midst of danger, his enemies constantly seeking his life. The news of the murder of Prince Edward reached Jasper Tudor at Tewkesbury, and he returned to Chepstow, taking with him Henry Tudor, now heir to the throne. At Chepstow they were unsuccessfully attacked by the Yorkist, Roger Vaughan, and retired to Pembroke Castle, where they were be-

176

sieged, but finally escaped to Brittany, where they remained for many years in exile. There let us leave them awhile, for Chepstow has a curious interest for the student of Shakespeare. Famous in the border history of Wales, it is notorious for the persistent search undertaken there by Dr. Orville Owen, the American champion of the Baconian theory. Dr. Owen declared that Bacon had secreted full proofs of his authorship, and that the supposed " cyphers " indicated the hiding-place of the documents. As Owen read these " cyphers," they referred him continually to a place called Striguil as the spot where the documents were hidden. On coming to England he learned that Striguil was a Norman corruption of the Welsh Ystraigl, by which name Chepstow was known to the early Welsh. Bacon, it was known, had lived awhile at Chepstow as the guest of the Earl of Pembroke. What more could a Baconian ask ? Only the final proof ! During these visits (the last in 1913), Dr. Owen spent hundreds of pounds in damming the bed of the Wye (by permission of the Duke of Beaufort) and excavating sites expected to yield the supposed *cache*.

Chepstow, it should be remembered, was in Henry's days in Wales. During the reign of his son, Monmouthshire was declared an English county for administrative purposes, but ecclesiastically it still remains in the diocese of Llandaff. The life of Monmouthshire is even yet thoroughly Welsh, so that Henry V. was most truly a Welshman, by early training if not by blood.

In connection with Bacon, we may mention here that Sir Hugh Evans' *Hang, hog,* and Mrs. Page's " Hang hog is Latin for bacon, I warrant you," is claimed by Sir Edwin Durning-Lawrence, Bart., as a part of the Baconian clue. The tale is told by Bacon himself of how a prisoner named Hog who had been condemned to death prayed for mercy on the score of kindred. " Ay," replied the Judge, " but you and I cannot be of kindred unless you are hanged: for Hog is not Bacon till it be well hanged." Nowhere has Lord Bacon indicated in his acknowledged works that he knew anything of Wales or the Welsh people, so that the present volume may provide the Baconians with an excuse for yet more tortuous ingenuity.

To return to the action of the play. The calamitous Wars of the Roses had resulted in the dethronement and ultimate assassination of Henry VI., and the capture and beheading, at Hereford, of Owen Tudor, who had actively espoused the Lancastrian cause.

178

Richard, Duke of Gloucester, who (according to the play) with his own hand murdered King Henry VI. and plotted the deaths of the two young Princes in the Tower, was the last of the Yorkist monarchs. In the realisation of his ambitious dreams he received vital assistance from the Duke of Buckingham, who was born at Brecon, the lordship of which had fallen to the Stafford family after the death of Sir David Gam. But after Richard's triumph he felt that he owed too much to Buckingham; and how he rewarded the unhappy Duke is shown in the following scene, which also reveals Richard's uneasy perception of the threatened rivalry of Harry Tudor of Richmond:

*Re-enter* BUCKINGHAM.

*Buck.* My lord, I have consider'd in my mind
The late demand that you did sound me in.*
   *K. Rich.* Well, let that pass. Dorset is fled to Richmond.
   *Buck.* I hear that news, my lord.
   *K. Rich.* Stanley, he is your wife's son: well, look to it.
   *Buck.* My lord, I claim the gift, my due by promise,
For which your honour and your faith is pawn'd;
The earldom of Hereford and the moveables
The which you promiséd I should possess.
   *K. Rich.* Stanley, look to your wife: if she convey
Letters to Richmond, you shall answer it.
   *Buck.* What says your highness to my just request?

---

\* Richard had asked him to undertake the assassination of the two young Princes.

*K. Rich.* As I remember Henry the Sixth
Did prophesy that Richmond should be king,
When Richmond was a little peevish boy.
A king, perhaps, perhaps,—
  *Buck.* My lord !
  *K. Rich.* How chance the prophet could not at that time
Have told me, I being by, that I should kill him ?
  *Buck.* My lord, your promise for the earldom,—
  *K. Rich.* Richmond ! When last I was at Exeter,
The mayor in courtesy show'd me the castle,
And call'd it Rougemont: at which name I started,
Because a bard of Ireland told me once,
I should not live long after I saw Richmond.
  *Buck.* My lord !
  *K. Rich.* Ay, what's o'clock ?
  *Buck.* I am thus bold to put your grace in mind
Of what you promised me.
  *K. Rich.*                   Well, but what's o'clock ?
  *Buck.* Upon the stroke of ten.
  *K. Rich.*                     Well, let it strike.
  *Buck.* Why let it strike ?
  *K. Rich.* Because that, like a Jack, thou keep'st the stroke
Betwixt thy begging and my meditation.
I am not in the giving vein to-day.
  *Buck.* Why, then resolve me whether you will or no.
  *K. Rich.* Tut, tut,
Thou troublest me; I am not in the vein.
                      *[Exeunt all but* BUCKINGHAM
  *Buck.* Is it even so ? rewards he my true service
With such deep contempt ? made I him king for this ?
O, let me think on Hastings, and be gone
To Brecknock, while my fearful head is on !       *[Exit.*

That " fearful head " was not to be saved, for all
its fears. Fighting under the standard of Richmond, Buckingham was captured by the Yorkists,

180

and Richard, his erstwhile master, sent him to the block without the slightest consideration for his past services.

With the news of Richmond's rising the action of the play of *Richard III.* quickens. Messengers bring Richard news of anti-Yorkist defections in various parts of the country, and the climax is reached when Stanley appears.

> *K. Rich.* How now, what news with you ?
> *Stan.* None good, my liege, to please you with the hearing;
> Nor none so bad, but it may well be told.
> *K. Rich.* Heyday, a riddle ! neither good nor bad !
> Why dost thou run so many mile about,
> When thou mayst tell thy tale a nearer way ?
> Once more, what news ?
> *Stan.*                      Richmond is on the seas.
> *K. Rich.* There let him sink, and be the seas on him !
> White-liver'd runagate, what doth he there ?
> *Stan.* I know not, mighty sovereign, but by guess.
> *K. Rich.* Well, sir, as you guess ?
> *Stan.* Stirr'd up by Dorset, Buckingham, and Ely,
> He makes for England, there to claim the crown.
> *K. Rich.* Is the chair empty ? is the sword unsway'd ?
> Is the king dead ? the empire unpossess'd ?
> What heir of York is there alive but we ?
> And who is England's king but great York's heir ?
> Then, tell me, what doth he upon the sea ?
> *Stan.* Unless for that, my liege, I cannot guess.
> *K. Rich.* Unless for that he comes to be your liege,
> You cannot guess wherefore the Welshman comes.
> Thou wilt revolt, and fly to him, I fear.
> *Stan.* No, mighty liege; therefore mistrust me not.

And in Scene 5 of the same act we learn that Richmond, long an exile in Brittany, has landed in Wales. Lord Stanley, in whose house the scene is laid, has heard that his son is a hostage. He is alone with Urswick, who, on being asked what followers the Tudor has, mentions the names of three Welshmen.

LORD STANLEY'S *House.*

*Stan.* Sir Christopher, tell Richmond this from me:
That in the sty of this most bloody boar
My son George Stanley is frank'd up in hold:
If I revolt, off goes young George's head;
The fear of that withholds my present aid.
But, tell me, where is princely Richmond now ?
   *Chris.* At Pembroke, or at Ha'rford-west, in Wales.
   *Stan.* What men of name resort to him ?
   *Chris.* Sir Walter Herbert, a renowned soldier;
Sir Gilbert Talbot, Sir William Stanley;
Oxford, redoubted Pembroke, Sir James Blunt,
And Rice ap Thomas, with a valiant crew;
And many more of noble fame and worth:
And towards London they do bend their course,
If by the way they be not fought withal.
   *Stan.* Return unto thy lord; commend me to him:
Tell him the queen hath heartily consented
He shall espouse Elizabeth her daughter.
These letters will resolve him of my mind.
Farewell.                      *[Exeunt.*

Richmond with his forces, which were largely Welsh, marched through Pembrokeshire and Cardiganshire, and encamped on Bosworth Field, where his rival was awaiting his coming. In the scene which represents the camps of the two opposing forces on the eve of the encounter we witness the troubled slumbers of Richard and the calm serenity of the sleep of Richmond.

" There is no creature loves me; and if I die no soul shall pity me," exclaims the agonised Richard, awaking from the terrible dreams in which his victims reproach him and foretell his doom. But Richmond passes the night in " the sweetest sleep and fairest-boding dreams."

Richmond is represented " as the chosen of God," the " destined avenger of the iniquities of Richard III."* That he so regards himself we gather from the inspiring oration which he delivers to his troops before the battle.

> God and our good cause fight upon our side;
> The prayers of holy saints and wronged souls,
> Like high-rear'd bulwarks, stand before our faces;
> Richard except, those whom we fight against
> Had rather have us win than him they follow:
> For what is he they follow? truly, gentlemen,
> A bloody tyrant and a homicide;
> One raised in blood, and one in blood establish'd;
> One that made means to come by what he hath,
> And slaughter'd those that were the means to help
>     him.
> A base foul stone, made precious by the foil

* Newell.

Of England's chair, where he is falsely set;
One that hath ever been God's enemy:
Then, if you fight against God's enemy,
God will in justice ward you as his soldiers. . . .
Then, in the name of God and all these rights,
Advance your standards, draw your willing swords.
God and Saint George! Richmond and victory! [*Exeunt.*

Then follows the defeat of Richard and the crowning of Richmond on the field of battle; and the new King, Henry VII., announces his intention of espousing Elizabeth of York, and so ending the civil strife between the Houses of York and Lancaster—a marriage which had actually been arranged, at Brecon, by Buckingham and the semi-captive Bishop of Ely.

" Henry the Seventh, a Welshman leading a Welsh army, had now become King of England. The prophecy that a Welshman was to be King of England, which had brought Llewellyn a crown of ivy and which had deceived Glendower, was at last fulfilled. The Welsh ceased to be rebels, and they entered heartily into the new life of the period, from its literature to its piracy " (Edwards).

Had Shakespeare dramatised the history of King Henry VII. we might have been told, in imperishable verse, of those remarkable events— some of the most remarkable in the history of the world—which occurred during the reign of the first Tudor monarch. His own career was not eventful; his activities were not spectacular, important though they were, and we must not forget that his legislative measures laid the foundations of England's greatness, and earned him the title of the " English Solomon "; but it was while he was on the throne that the two Americas were discovered, the sea route to India was opened, printing was introduced into England, and the revival of learning commenced, while British merchants began to lay the foundations of the future British Empire by trading with foreign parts.

The loyalty of Wales to the English throne was consolidated in the reign of King Henry VIII., who in the preamble to his Act of Union between England and Wales spoke of the singular love which he had for the Welsh people. In the reign of Elizabeth the bonds of union were drawn closer still. Henry VIII., although the possessor of many of the virtues, as well as most of the less agreeable characteristics, of the Welsh people, was essentially an English Prince. We shall not, therefore, consider the play of *Henry VIII.* as being one of those which illustrate Shakespeare's opinions of the Welsh nation, although it may be accepted as a glorification of the Tudor monarchy.

# CHAPTER XIV

## SHAKESPEARE'S *SONNETS* AND "MR. W. H."

THERE are certain circumstances connected with Shakespeare's *Sonnets* and their publication which have a special interest for the Welsh reader. When the theatres were closed, owing to the plague, in 1592-93, Shakespeare, no longer absorbed by his labours as dramatist of a busy theatrical company, made his first appeal to the reading public. In 1593 he published *Venus and Adonis*, which was dedicated to his friend and patron, Henry Wriothesley, the third Earl of Southampton. In 1594 *Lucrece* made its appearance, and about this time Shakespeare is assumed to have begun the writing of his *Sonnets*. He did not print them then, however; until 1609 they remained in private circulation. Meres, writing in 1598, speaks of Shakespeare's " sugar'd Sonnets among his private friends," and two of the *Sonnets* figured in Jaggard's *Passionate Pilgrim*, published in 1599. On May 20th, 1609, " a book called Shakespeare's Sonnettes " was entered on the Stationers' Register by Thomas Thorpe (who had served his apprenticeship with a printer named Richard Watkins), and in the same year the Quarto edition appeared, bearing the title " Shakespeare's Sonnets. Never before Imprinted At London by G. Eld for T. T. [Thomas Thorpe], and to be solde by William Apsley, 1609." It is believed that the publication took place without the sanction of the author; at all events, the dedication is not his, but Thorpe's. It runs as follows:

TO THE · ONLIE · BEGETTER · OF ·
THESE · INSVING · SONNETS ·
MR. W. H. ALL · HAPPINESSE ·
AND · THAT · ETERNITE ·
PROMISED ·
BY ·
OVR EVER LIVING POET ·
WISHETH ·
THE WELL WISHING ·
ADVENTURER · IN ·
SETTING ·
FORTH.

T. T.

Two controversies have arisen around the wording of this dedication. The first of these is concerned with the identification of " Mr. W. H." and the second with the meaning to be ascribed to the word " begetter." Many notable Shakespearian scholars are satisfied that " Mr. W. H." was intended to refer to William Herbert, third Earl of Pembroke, of the second creation, who was born in 1580 and

187

died in 1630, and that the word " begetter " was
used by Thorpe in the sense of " inspirer," the
inference being that Lord William Herbert was the
" sole inspirer " of the *Sonnets*. Sir Sidney Lee, however, is emphatically of opinion that the " W. H."
whom Thorpe desired to honour was a Mr. Wm. Hall,
a bookseller's assistant, who was professionally
engaged, like Thorpe, in procuring works for publication, and that the word " begetter " in the
dedication must be taken as meaning " procurer."
Two further suggestions have been made with
reference to the cryptic letters " W. H." One is
that they were intended as a covert allusion to
Henry Wriothesley, the Earl of Southampton
(the initials of his name having been purposely
transposed); and the other that they refer to Sir
William Hervey, the third husband of Southampton's mother. This latter suggestion is made by
Fleay, who adds : " She died in 1607, and I conjecture that the delay in publishing the Sonnets was
due to the fact that she wished them to remain
in MS., at any rate during her lifetime, and the
copy used may have been found among her papers."
But this theory, like many of Fleay's hypotheses,
is ingenious rather than plausible.

The Herbert theory was first advanced by James
Boaden, the biographer of Kemble and Mrs. Siddons,

in the *Gentleman's Magazine* for 1832; but Hunter claims that Bright had previously come to a similar conclusion, and cites the following letter, addressed to him by Bright:

" It is now more than thirteen years, in 1819, since I detailed to you the progress of the discovery I had made that William Herbert, third Earl of Pembroke, was undoubtedly the person to whom Shakespeare addressed his first 126 sonnets. Another friend, Dr. Holme of Manchester, had been informed of my secret a year earlier."

One prominent Welsh supporter of the Herbert theory is Sir Owen M. Edwards, who writes, in his *Story of Wales*:

" Sir Henry Sidney's famous children—Philip and Mary—spent most of their childhood at Ludlow. Mary married Henry, Earl of Pembroke, and it was at their home at Wilton that Philip Sidney wrote his *Arcadia*. Henry succeeded his father-in-law and father as President of the Court of Wales. He had shown already in a magnificent feast at Cardiff that his policy was one of conciliatory moderation. Like his wife, he was a patron of learning, and he threw himself with ardour into the activity and hopes of that time of discovery of worlds and truths. When the sixteenth century came to an end Elizabeth was still wielding the

189

sceptre of England, and at the Court of Wales there ruled Mary Herbert, whom Spenser described as ' the ornament of womankind,' *whose youthful beauty Shakespeare saw mirrored in her son*, and of whom Ben Jonson wrote:

> Death ! ere thou hast slain another
> Wise and fair and good as she,
> Time shall throw a dart at thee."

The italics are ours. The allusion is to the following lines:

> Thou art thy mother's glass, and she in thee
> Calls back the lovely April of her prime.

It might be objected that there is no allusion: that the mother is merely the third term in the argument; but if no specific allusion had been intended it would have been more natural—at all events, more logical—to mention the father of the person apostrophied.

" If a number of the Sonnets—principally 1-26," says Elze — " must absolutely be considered as addressed to one of the two Earls, it would seem as if there was more reason for supposing the subject to have been the Earl of Pembroke than Southampton. The Earl of Pembroke was first of all a great admirer and patron of poetry, to whom numerous works and poems were dedicated (among others Ben Jonson's *Catiline*, 1616). That he was disinclined to marry is proved by a letter of Rowland White to Sir Robert Sidney (1599), where he says of Pembroke, ' I don't find any disposition at all in this gallant young Lord to marry.' Pembroke was throughout his life considered a voluptuary. Davies, too, in one of his Sonnets urges him to marry (in *Wit's Pilgrimage*)." Pembroke finally married in 1603.

Thomas Tyler, who reasoned on the same lines as Boaden, agreed with Shaw, Harris, and other modern writers in identifying the " dark lady " of the second group of *Sonnets* as Mary Fitton, a lady of Elizabeth's Court, who became the mistress of the Earl of Pembroke. If we accept the conclusion of Wordsworth, that the *Sonnets* were the key to Shakespeare's heart, and the identification of the youth as Wm. Herbert and the " dark lady " as Mistress Fitton, it follows that we find in the *Sonnets* a real and tragic love-story, which must have reacted on the poet's outlook on life. The *Sonnets* are usually divided into two groups. In the first group the poet beseeches a beautiful youth to marry, in order that his youth and good looks may be perpetuated in his children, and makes many protestations of his devotion to the object of his appeal. We then find that the youth has won the affections of the poet's mistress in the absence of the obscurer lover, and although the poet forgives the double betrayal, he recognises that he must now lose both friend and mistress. In the second group he describes the lady as possessing a dark complexion and raven black hair and eyes, and denounces her for having beguiled his friend. Sir Sidney Lee, in rejecting the Fitton surmise, quotes the statement made by Lady Newdegate in her *Gossip from a Muniment Room* (1897) that two well-preserved portraits of Mary Fitton at Arbury show her to have been a lady of fair complexion with brown hair and grey eyes.

The "Herbert" theorists furthermore claim that the "punning" *Sonnets* indicate that the name of Shakespeare's friend was the same as his own. The first of these *Sonnets* is number cxxxv.

> Whoever hath her wish, thou hast thy *Will*,
> And *Will* to boot, and *Will* in overplus. . . .

Sonnet cxxxvi. contains the lines:

> If thy soul check thee that I come so near,
> Swear to thy blind soul that I was thy *Will*. . . .
> Make but my name thy love, and love that still,
> And then thou lov'st me—for my name is *Will*.

While Sonnet cxliii. concludes:

> So will I pray that thou mayst have thy *Will*,
> If thou turn back, and my loud crying still.

The italics appear in the Quarto, and Tyrwhitt suggests that the lines refer to a "Mr. William

Hughes," as in the seventh line of the twentieth sonnet in the first edition, the word "Hews" (hues) is in italics, and begins with a capital: "A man of hew, all *Hews* in his controwling."

In recent years the Herbert theory seems to have secured the largest number of adherents.

William Jaggard, the publisher, in 1599 issued a collection of poems bearing the title of "The Passionate Pilgrim by W. Shakespeare." Only two copies of this work are known to be in existence. There are twenty poems in the volume, but the experts have decided that only five are by Shakespeare. These five are Nos. 1, 2, 3, 5, and 16. The four sonnets (Nos. 4, 6, 9, and 11) are credited to Bartholomew Griffin, who died in 1602. Mr. Pym Yeatman's "Griffin Pedigree" shows him to have been of Welsh descent and a cousin of Shakespeare. We hear of him at Bidford in 1582. "There can be little doubt," writes Mr. Yeatman, "that the two poets, William Shakespeare and Bartholomew Griffin, kept up their kinship in blood and in letters both in Warwickshire and amongst the wits of London, since their poems became so intermixed that the true authorship was not properly known. Griffin wrote some exquisite poetry . . . much in the same style as that of William Shakespeare, and the pirate publishers may almost be excused for confounding them." As a matter of fact, his verse may be distinguished from Shakespeare by its very frankly sensuous and fleshly tone.

Bartholomew Griffin's collection of Sonnets, bearing the title of " Fidessa more Chaste than Kind," was printed in 1596 " by the Widow Orwin for Matthew Lownes," and is dedicated " To the most kind and virtuous Gentleman Master William Essex of Lamebourne in the County of Berk[shire] Esquire." Of Bartholomew Griffin Mrs. Stopes writes: " He might have been one of the Griffins of Dingley, or the son of Mr. Ralph Griffin, the preacher of Warwick, who went out with the Town Council to meet the Queen in her progress thither in 1571, preached a sermon on ' Christian Warfare,' and gave her some Latin verses. The Queen ' caused her coach to be opened every part and side that they might see her.' The people let off fireworks in their rejoicing, which burned four houses to the ground and caused great consternation. After great sport at Kenilworth she went to Charlecote, to the Lord Compton, on her return, an occasion on which Stratford would doubtless pour forth to meet her." If Shakespeare was one of the spectators he was only seven years of age. It is more likely that his first sight of Elizabeth would have been at Kenilworth in 1575.

194

# CHAPTER XV

## SHAKESPEARE'S " PUCK " AND THE WELSH " PWCCA "

THERE was formerly a very real and widespread belief in fairies among the people of Wales, and the belief still lingers in some of the more rural parts of the Principality. Many were the tales told from village to village of little sprites seen dancing in the meadows on moonlight nights, and the Tylwyth Teg, or fairy family, was regarded with mingled feelings of affection and awe. There were good fairies and bad fairies, but there was also another kind of fairy, neither good nor bad, but simply mischievous, and him the old Welsh people knew as Pwcca. In Shakespeare's play, *A Midsummer Night's Dream*, we have a " merry wanderer of the night" who is given the name of "Puck."

> That frights the maidens of the villagery;
> Skim milk, and sometimes labour in the quern,
> And bootless make the breathless housewife churn,
> And sometime make the drink to bear no barm,
> Mislead night wanderers, laughing at their harm. . . .

195

It may be noted, too, that there is a *pauky* in Scotland, a *pooca* in Ireland, and in Iceland—where many Irish bards either settled, or were taken as prisoners—there is a *puki*.

We are told that Shakespeare was the first to use the general term of " Puck " as a proper name, and some Welshmen of letters claim that Shakespeare's " Puck " was suggested by the little Welsh fairy Pwcca. In his *British Goblins* Wirt Sikes states the case for Pwcca so concisely that we cannot do better than quote his arguments:

" Shakespeare's use of Welsh folklore, it should be noted, was extensive, and particularly faithful. Keightly, in his *Fairy Mythology*, rates the bard soundly for his inaccurate use of fairy mythology. But the reproach will not apply as regards Wales. From his Welsh informant Shakespeare got Mab, which is simply the Cymric for a little child, and the root of numberless words signifying ' babyish, childish, love of children (Mabgar), kitten (Mabgath), prattling (Mabrarth),' and, most notable of all, of ' Mabinogion.' " Proceeding, the same writer remarks: " There is a Welsh tradition to the effect that Shakespeare received his knowledge of Cambrian fairies from his friend Richard Price, son of Sir John Price of the Priory, Brecon. It is even claimed that Cwm Pwcca, or Puck Valley, a part of the romantic glen of the Clydach in Breconshire, is the original scene of the *Midsummer Night's Dream*, a fancy as light and airy as Puck himself. Anyhow, there Cwm Pwcca is, and in the sylvan days before Frère and Powell's ironworks were set up there it is said to have been as full of goblins as a Methodist's head is full of piety. And there are in Wales other places bearing like names, where Pwcca's pranks are well remembered by old inhabitants. The range given in Wales to the popular fancy is expressed with fidelity by Shakespeare's words in the mouth of Puck:

> I'll follow you, I'll lead you about, around,
> Through bog, through bush, through brake, through
> briar.
> Sometime a horse I'll be, sometime a hound,
> A hog, a headless bear, sometime a fire;
> And neigh, and bark, and grunt, and roar, and burn
> Like horse, hound, hog, bear, fire, at every turn."

In this connection it is curious to note that in one of the later poems of Welsh mediæval literature Gwion Bach transforms himself into a hare, a bird, a fish, and a grain of wheat; while similar transformations occur in early Irish poetry.

According to a letter written by the poet Campbell to Mrs. Fletcher in 1833, and published in her autobiography, it was thought that Shakespeare visited the valley of Cwm Pwcca in person. " It is no later than yesterday," wrote Campbell, "that I discovered a probability, almost near a certainty, that Shakespeare visited friends in the very town (Brecon in Wales) where Mrs. Siddons was born, and that he there found in a neighbouring glen called ' The Valley of Fairy Puck ' the principal machinery for his *Midsummer Night's Dream*." Campbell's probability, unfortunately for us, does not appear to have materialised into a certainty.

In this connection Sir Sidney Lee remarks (July 5th, 1917): " I have not been able so far to discover any foundation for the statement that Richard Price of Brecon was a friend of Shakespeare. The allegation seems to rest on no more obvious basis than that which makes the dramatist's mother of Welsh descent." As we have seen, however, it was from his father that he derived the Welsh blood that flowed in his veins.

The theory of Shakespeare's supposed connection with Brecon seems to have originated with the Breconshire county historian, Theophilus Jones, who was influenced by the fact that one Hugh Evans, who was Rector of Merthyr Cynog in Breconshire, and whose executor was Mr. Richard Price of the Priory, Brecon, bore the same name as the schoolmaster-parson in the *Merry Wives of Windsor* (see Chapter IV., p. 53). "Carnhuanawc" (the Rev. Thomas Price), author of *Hanes Cymry*, was much with Theophilus Jones in his youth, and communicated this idea to Thomas Campbell, who had some correspondence with the Rev. Thomas Price when writing his *Life of Mrs. Siddons*. (The celebrated actress was born in 1755 at a house in High Street, Brecon, now known as the Siddons Wine Vaults, but then called the Shoulder of Mutton.)

Fleay, in his *Chronicle History of the Life and Work of William Shakespeare*, speaking of the first quarto of the *Merry Wives of Windsor*, tells us that Sir Hugh Evans in the fairy scene appears as "Puck Hobgoblin" in black. "The prefixes *Qu.*, *Qui.*, and *Pist.*," he says, "are mistakes for *Queen* and *Puck*. Pistol and Quickly cannot be actors in this scene, nor in the entrance are they placed with 'Evans, Anne Page, Fairies,' but at the ends of the second and third lines, as if by after-thought. All the Pistol fairy speeches belong to Evans (Puck). There seems to have arisen some confusion in the final revision when this scene was probably altered."

In the modern versions of the play, Anne Page, as the Fairy Queen, calls upon "crier Hobgoblin"

199

to " make the fairy o-yes," and the speech of Hobgoblin—which is interrupted by Falstaff's aside—
is continued by Evans. But in the middle of the
scene Hobgoblin and Evans have one line of verse
divided between them. This looks as if Hobgoblin
was originally a separate character, especially as
Evans is described as a Satyr. Query: who takes
the part of Hobgoblin? William, apparently. It
is by no means clear that Fleay is right in saying
that confusion has arisen in the final revision;
yet it is certainly curious that both Hobgoblin
and Evans act as the fairy crier.

The music of the Tylwyth Teg has been variously
described by those who claim to have heard it,
but usually with much vagueness, as " a sweet
intangible harmony, recalling the words of Caliban
in *The Tempest* (Act III., Scene 3)"

> The isle is full of noises,
> Sounds and sweet airs that give delight and hurt not.

In *A Winter's Tale* an essentially Celtic note is
struck. The old Shepherd, in Act III., Scene 2,
declares:

> This is fairy gold, boy, and 'twill prove so;
> Up with't, keep it close; home, home, the next way.
> We are lucky, boy, and to be so still requires nothing
> but secrecy.

200

We have here, as Sikes points out, a traditional belief of the Welsh peasantry in a nutshell. Welsh, Cornish, and Irish fairy lore is full of stories of the fairy gold that vanishes, or turns to withered leaves, if the condition of secrecy is not observed by the finder.

# CHAPTER XVI

## CONTEMPORARY WELSH PRINTERS AND PUBLISHERS

SIXTEEN of Shakespeare's plays were printed during his lifetime, but Shakespeare had no hand in their publication. As explained in Chapter II., the printing of plays was regarded by the shareholders in theatrical ventures as inimical to the interests of the stage. Publishers, however, were not, in Shakespeare's days, hampered by restrictions as to copyright; they accordingly printed successful plays when they could obtain copies, whether from actors or from shorthand writers who attended the performances in order to obtain the text. In 1600 the first quarto of *The Merchant of Venice* was published. It was issued from the press of a Welsh printer named James Roberts, who had a printing-house in the Barbican. In the same year he published also the second quarto of *Titus Andronicus*, and in 1604 the second quarto of *Hamlet*. For nearly twenty years Roberts enjoyed the privilege of printing the " players' bills " and programmes, and must almost certainly

have come into contact with Shakespeare in a business capacity. In 1606 Roberts' printing business
was acquired by William Jaggard, the publisher
of *The Passionate Pilgrim;* and it was from the
press of Roberts, thus acquired, that William
Jaggard, with two of Shakespeare's friends and
fellow-actors, John Heminges and Henry Condell,
issued, in 1623, the celebrated First Folio, or first
edition of Shakespeare's collected plays. In 1619
Jaggard published reprints of *A Midsummer
Night's Dream* and *The Merchant of Venice,* but he
antedated them by nineteen years, and gave the
name of the printer as James Roberts. On the title
page of each of these reprinted quartos was the same
engraved device as that employed by Roberts—
a carnation with the Welsh motto " Heb Ddieu :
Heb Ddim " (Without God : without anything).
It has been discovered that this device was first
used by a London printer named Richard Jones
about the year 1592. When Jones ceased to use
it is not definitely known, but it passed into the
possession of William Jaggard, who used it in
1610, and in whose printing-house it was afterwards
employed up to the time of the Civil War by himself
and his successors, the Cotes family. Mr. Harry
Farr, the Chief Librarian at Cardiff, who has been
investigating the history of this device, has found

that after the Civil War it was occasionally used by the Cotes family and their successors, and in the early years of the eighteenth century it was employed by Edward Powell, another Welshman, on the title page of the first edition of Ellis Wynne's *Bardd Cwsg*. In the panels of the device appear the letters R. I. (indicating Richard Jones). "The Roberts Jaggard-Cotes and Clark Press," writes Mr. Farr, "was founded by John Charlewood at the sign of the Half Eagle and Key in the Barbican about 1562, and it easily surpasses in interest and continuity every other concerned in the printing of the works of Shakespeare."

Gollancz gives a number of interesting details regarding the first and second quartos of *Hamlet*. The authorised text of *Hamlet*, he tells us, is based upon (1) the quarto edition printed in the year 1604 by James Roberts, and (2) the First Folio version of 1623. The 1604 edition is generally known as the Second Quarto, to distinguish it from a remarkable production of the previous year "printed for N. L. and John Trundell." The printer's name is not given, but the following entry appeared in the Stationers' Register under the date 1602, " xxvj. to Juli j.":

" *James Robertes* entered for his Copie vnder the handes of Master *Pasfield* and master *Waterson*

Warden A booke called ' *the Revenge of* HAMLETT *Prince [of] Denmarke' as yt was lateli Acted by the Lord Chamberleyne his servantes* . . . vjd."

James Roberts, who was the printer of the 1604 edition, may also have been in Professor Gollancz' opinion the printer of the quarto of 1603, and this entry may have referred to the projected publication. On the other hand, this entry may have been made by Roberts in order to secure the play for himself, and some " inferior and nameless " printer may have anticipated him by the publication of an imperfect, surreptitious, and garbled version, which impudently offered as Shakespeare's such wretched stuff as this :

> To be, or not to be, I there's the point,
> To Die, to sleepe, is that all: I all ?
> No, to sleepe, to dream I mary there it goes,
> For in that dreame of death, when wee awake,
> And borne before an e'erlasting Judge;
> From whence no passenger ever return'd,
> The undiscovered country, at whose sight
> The happy smile and the accursed damn'd.

In all probability the shorthand notes of an incompetent stenographer, taken during the performance of the play, formed the basis of the printer's " copy " of the 1603 quarto.

Among the quarto editions of non-Shakespearian plays performed by Shakespeare's company are the following, which were entered in the Stationers' Register:

1593-94. January 7: Entered for R. Jones *A Knack to Know a Knave*.

(A date between 1595 and 1599). Entered for W. Jones *Mucedorus*.

1600. May 27: Entered for J. Roberts *Cloth breeches and velvet hose*.

1600. May 29: Entered for J. Roberts *Alarum to London*.

In the year 1600 a publisher of music named Robert Jones (whose name suggests a Welsh origin) issued a *First Booke of Songs and Ayres*, and in the collection is a concerted vocal piece with lute accompaniment entitled "Corydon's Farewell to Phillis." The words of the song are not by Shakespeare, but they are sung, with various alterations in the words, by Sir Toby Belch and the Clown in their drunken scene in *Twelfth Night* (Act II., Scene 3) as follows:

*Malvolio*. Sir Toby, I must be round with you. My lady bade me tell you, that though she harbours you as her kinsman, she's nothing ally'd to your disorders. If you can separate your selfe and your misdemeanours, you are welcome to the house; if not, and it would please you to take your leave of her, she is very willing to bid you farewell.

*Sir Toby*. *Farewell, dear heart, since I must needs be gone.*
*Maria*. Nay, good Sir Toby.
*Clown*. *His eyes do show his days are almost done.*

*Malvolio.* Is't even so ?
*Sir Toby. But I will never die.*
*Clown.* Sir Toby, there you lie.
*Malvolio.* This is much credit to you.
*Sir Toby. Shall I bid him go ?*
*Clown. What, and if you do ?*
*Sir Toby. Shall I bid him go, and spare not ?*
*Clown. O no, no, no, no, you dare not.*
*Sir Toby.* Out o' time, sir ? ye lye.   Art any more than a
steward ?  Dost thou think, because thou art virtuous, there
shall be no more cakes and ale ?

The first two of the five stanzas may be given
to illustrate the text:

> *Corydon's Farewell to Phillis.*
>
> Farewell, dear love, since thou wilt needs be gone,
> Mine eyes do show my life is almost done.
> > Nay, I will never die
> > So long as I can spie
> > There be many mo'
> > Tho' that she do goe,
> There be many mo', I fear not,
> Why then let her goe, I care not.
>
> Farewell, farewell; since this I find is true,
> I will not spend more time in wooing you;
> > But I will seek elsewhere
> > If I may find love there.
> > Shall I bid her goe ?
> > What an' if I doe ?
> Shall I bid her goe and spare not ?
> O no, no, no, no, I dare not.

Of Robert Jones's career very little is known.
Mr. W. Barclay Squire, in his introduction to
a reprint (published in 1901) of *The Muses Gardin*

*for Delights: or the fift Booke of Ayres: Composed by Robert Jones*, is unable to tell us more of the composer than that on April 29th, 1597, a grace was passed for his degree of Mus.Bac. at Oxford, in which it is stated that he studied music for sixteen years, and was a member of St. Edmund's Hall. In 1615 (according to Collier's *Annals of the Stage*, 1879) a Privy Seal for patent was granted Philip Rosseter, Philip Kingman, Robert Jones, and Ralph Reeve, who had bought ground and buildings near Puddle Wharf, Blackfriars, on which to erect a theatre. The building which the partners had acquired was " called by the name of the Ladie Saunders House, or otherwise the Porter's Hall," and was then in the occupation of Robert Jones. The scheme met with great opposition, and when the building was nearly completed the Lord Mayor, by the King's authority, ordered that it should be made unfit for use as a theatre, and the order was executed in three days' time.

In 1610 Shakespeare, Burbage, and their five colleagues had come into possession of the Blackfriars Theatre, and were presumably inimical to the attempt made by Robert Jones and his colleagues to erect a rival theatre at Puddle Wharf, Blackfriars.

Among those to whom Jones dedicated his works

were Henry, Prince of Wales, Robert Sidney, and Robert Cecil, Earl of Salisbury. The authorship of *Corydon and Phillis* remains in doubt. There is also a doubt as to the date of the first production of *Twelfth Night*, and the question arises as to whether it was produced before or after the issue in 1600 of Robert Jones's *Booke of Songs and Ayres*. The earliest appearance of the play in print was in the First Folio of 1623, but Manningham, a barrister of the Middle Temple, mentions in his diary, under the date February 2nd, 1601-02, that " at our feast we had a play called *Twelue Night, or What you Will*." This is the earliest definite evidence we have of the production of the play, but Shakespearian investigators have collected several items of collateral significance. A Latin version of the Italian play from which Shakespeare obtained the central idea of *Twelfth Night* was produced at Cambridge in 1590 and 1598, while an Italian company may have produced the original at Windsor in 1577-78. An interesting article on Shakespeare's knowledge of Italy and Italian, by Sir Edward Sullivan, in the *Nineteenth Century and After* for February, 1918, proves conclusively that *Twelfth Night* was based on *Gl'Ingannati*, produced in Siena in 1531, and brought to England by Italian players. This article is note-

14

worthy for showing how quickly and accurately Shakespeare assimilated facts relating to countries which he had not visited. Even when he has been held by many commentators to have made absurd mistakes it now appears that he was right, and they wrong. His knowledge of foreign languages, etc., has been cited as a proof—to be Irish—that he was Bacon. But this is absurd: on these lines a critic of the future might claim that Kipling must have been a soldier, sailor, member of the I.C.S., engineer, aeronaut, painter, chemist, etc. Genius is an infinite capacity for assimilation.

Mr. Morton Luce points out that in 1599 Sir Robert Shirley returned from his embassy to the Shah—or Sophy—of Persia, to which we find a reference in Act II., Scene 5, of the play. In the same year was printed the first edition of Morley's *Consort Lessons*, which contained the song (believed, however, to have been written by Shakespeare), " O mistress mine, where are you roaming?" which is sung by the Clown in *Twelfth Night*. The year 1599 also saw the publication of " the new map of the Indies " bound up with copies of Hakluyt, and evidently alluded to in Act III., Scene 2, of the play. The words " bibble-babble " (Act IV., Scene 2) might also have been taken from Dr. Harsnet's *Discovery of the Fraudulent Practices of*

*John Darrel* (1599), where they are given some prominence, and it is pointed out that in 1600 the Privy Council issued an injunction which may have prompted the anti-Puritanical allusions of Sir Andrew Aguecheek in Act II., Scene 3, and Act III., Scene 2. These topical allusions in the play are regarded by some commentators as tending to fix the date of the first production of the play as the autumn of 1599, but Welsh students incline to the opinion that Robert Jones's musical setting popularised the song, with the result that it attracted the attention of Shakespeare.

# CHAPTER XVII

## WALES IN THE SIXTEENTH CENTURY

BEFORE the coming of the Tudors, Wales was, to the English, a hostile country. Peace ensued with the Tudor accession, and the country received a considerable degree of legislative relief during the reign of Henry VIII., who practically repealed all the former penal statutes by his Act of Union between England and Wales. This Act ordained that all Welshmen should have equal rights and privileges with Englishmen; that Welshmen and Englishmen, being equally the subjects of the King, should rank equally before the laws of the United Kingdom. The importance of this Act to Welshmen will be better understood when we take a glance at the provisions of some of the Acts passed in the reign of Henry IV. By 2 Henry IV., c. xii. (see *A Picture of Wales during the Tudor Period*, Nevins), a full-blooded Welshman born in Wales of a Welsh father and Welsh mother might not purchase lands or houses in certain mercantile towns adjoining the marches, and no Welshman might be harboured or received so as to become a citizen or burgess of such town. In the same year three more statutes were enacted providing that if any Welshman should steal cattle from an Englishman and not return them within seven days after demand the Englishman might take the law into his own hands, and steal the Welshman's cattle. By 2 Henry IV., c. xix., no Englishman could be condemned at the suit of a Welshman in Wales except by English justices, and by subsequent Acts no Welshman was allowed to carry arms, or possess cattle, or fortify his house, and no Welshman could hold any kind of office, as lawyer, sheriff, constable or the like. A great injustice affecting women was also perpetrated by 4 Henry IV., c. xxxiv., which ran as follows: " It is enacted that no Englishman married to a Welsh woman either friendly or allianced to Owen ap Glendowry, traitor to our lord the king, or to any Welshwoman since the rebellion of the said Owen, or who in time to come shall be married to any Welshwoman, shall be put into any office in Wales or in the marches of the same."

All these iniquitous Acts were swept away by King Henry VIII., who, being a Welshman himself, strongly disapproved of them.

When King Henry came to the throne, however, there was still trouble in the marches of Wales.

" Neither life nor property was safe there," writes Finnemore (*Social Life in Wales*). " Sir John Wynn, of Gwydir, in the County of Carnarvon, was born in 1553, in the latter part of the Tudor period. He wrote a book, in which he set down things he remembered, and things he had been told of the days before he was born. He shows us Wales in the early part of the sixteenth century, full of strife and disorder, in which every man seemed to be against his neighbour, and battle, murder, and sudden death were the ordinary events of everyday life. The strife between kinsmen was often far more savage and bitter than between strangers, and Sir John tells us that when an ancestor left Eifionydd to settle in Vantconway, a district swarming with robbers and fugitives from the law, he explained his reasons for the change by saying ' that he should find elbow room in that vast country among the bondmen' [servants who had fled from their lords], and that he had rather fight with outlaws and thieves than with his own blood and kindred, ' for if I live in mine own house in Eifionydd I must either kill my own kinsmen or be killed by them.' Among these proud and fiery Welshmen the motive of a murderous feud was often of the most trifling nature. Nine times out of ten it lay in a question of rank and dignity, who should have the highest place at a feast, who should have the right to the first good-morrows; some matter, small in itself, but bringing to the fore all the stiffness of family pride and the resolution to avenge an insult, whether real or fancied."

Toward the close of the Tudor period the spirit of litigation obsessed the Welsh people, and there was a continuous stream of litigants to Ludlow to demand justice from the great court of Wales. Luckily at that time there was a good man and a lover of justice as President of the Court. His name was Sir Henry Sidney, whose family became closely associated with Wales. His daughter Mary married Henry, Earl of Pembroke. His son, Sir Philip Sidney, was " the jewel of Elizabeth's reign," known to every schoolboy for his conduct on the field of Zutphen, where he was mortally wounded, and behaved with a chivalry that made his name famous. His *Arcadia* is one of our literary treasures. Sir Philip, we learn from the *Stradling Correspondence*, was an admirer of the Welsh harp, or, as it was quaintly called, " the instrument with wyars."

" The fray of Montague and Capulet," says Mr. W. Dircks, " Shakespeare could draw from actual scenes he witnessed in the streets of London." He was living at the time of Lord Herbert of

Cherbury's fierce encounter with Sir John Ayres in Whitehall, and doubtless heard of it.

These were the days of duels and hare-brained affrays and escapades, not only in London, but also in Wales. For the details of one skirmish which happened in South Wales in the lifetime of Shakespeare, and which may be considered as typical of others constantly occurring in the Principality, we turn once more to Finnemore's interesting work.

On Sunday, October 9th, 1596, there was a great affray at Llantwit Major, which shows how a turbulent gentleman could keep a whole neighbourhood in terror of him. On that Sunday morning two great families named Van and Seys, between whom there was no love lost, went to service at Llantwit Church. Edmund Van and his servants arrived at church armed to the teeth; the Seys family, not expecting trouble, had left their weapons at home. When the Vans went into church they found William Thomas, a servant of the Seys family, seated in a pew alone, saying his prayers. Perhaps William had got into a Van pew; perhaps the Vans were only looking for an excuse to start a disturbance, but two of the Van servants went into the pew, caught hold of William Thomas, and began to knock his head against the wall,

216

while Edmund Van stood in the aisle and remarked severely: " Sirrah William Thomas, thou art a saucy Jacke; that is not thy place." Peace, however, was made for the moment, and the service went on. After church the Vans were the first out and beset the great door, waiting for the Seys people. There was a savage scuffle at the church door, and the Vans attacked their enemies with sword and dagger, driving them back into the sacred building. The assailed party escaped from the church by another door, and fled into the town and took refuge in the house of Hopkin ap Rees. The Vans marched through the town with weapons drawn, creating a great uproar, abusing and beating all who dared to resist them, and, in trying to restore order, the parish constable was struck down and severely wounded. As the constable lay on the ground he heard Edmund Van coming up to the place and shouting, " Kill him ! kill them all !" The constable struggled to his feet, and managed to gain the house of Hopkin ap Rees, where he found shelter among the other fugitives. The latter stood in the utmost danger until word was sent to Sir Edward Stradling of St. Donats, who gathered a strong force of well-armed retainers, and came at their head to put down the riot and drive away the Vans.

The records of the Court of Star Chamber, the famous tribunal of Tudor times, give us other vivid and striking pictures of feuds and encounters among the Welshmen of the time.

The religious condition of Wales during the Tudor period was very dark. " The gentry and the wealthy," said Rev. Griffith Roberts, who wrote at the time, "are without thought of faith in the world "; but matters improved in the reign of Queen Elizabeth, who in 1563 obtained the passing of an Act of Parliament which ordered a translation to be made into vernacular Welsh of the Old and New Testaments, and also of the English Prayer Book, under a heavy penalty for delay, amounting (so Nevins informs us) to nearly a quarter of the value of some of the Bishoprics. In the Preamble to the Act Elizabeth explained that she did this " that thereby Her Highness's most loving subjects, understanding in their own language the terrible and fearful threatenings of God against the wicked and malefactors; the pleasant and infallible promises made to the elect and chosen flock with a just order to rule and guide their lives according to the Commandments of God, might much better learn to love and fear their neighbours, which book being received as a most precious jewel with unspeakable joy of all such her subjects as did not understand the *English* tongue, the which tongue is *not* understanded by the greatest number of Her Majesty's most loving and obedient subjects inhabiting the country of *Wales*, who therefore are utterly destituted of God's holy word and do remain in the like or rather more darkness and ignorance than they were in the time of the papistry; be it therefore enacted that," etc. Elizabeth did for Wales in this respect what no King or Queen has ever done for Scotland or for Ireland. "In her days," wrote Shakespeare, "God shall be truly known."

## CHAPTER XVIII

### SCENES IN WHICH THE WELSH CHARACTERS APPEAR

THE following chapter contains a synopsis of all the scenes of Shakespeare's plays in which Welsh characters (as apart from British or Celtic) play a sustained part. We shall not refer again to *Richard II.* or the third part of *King Henry VI.*, or to *Richard III.*, as the Welsh scenes or characters in these plays are sufficiently noticed in Chapters VIII. and XIII. The scenes in question are here dealt with from the standpoint of their contents and action, whereas they have hitherto been considered in respect of character and allusions to Welsh tradition. A certain reduplication being inevitable, the unleisured reader may proceed directly to the *Conclusions* which brings this volume to a close.

### 1. " KING HENRY IV." (FIRST PART).

It is worthy of note that the first part of *King Henry IV.*, in which Glendower plays a significant part, is the first of the plays in which Shakespeare makes an extensive use of prose. In his early plays there is a free use of rhyme, but as his taste matured he realised that blank verse and prose were better adapted to his purpose. For his historical facts Shakespeare, or the writer of the original version, if it be true that the Histories are chronicle-plays revised and expanded by Shakespeare, relied principally upon Holinshed, but he appears to have obtained a hint for Prince Hal and his dissolute companions from an older piece entitled *The Famous Victories of Henry V., containing the Honourable Battle of Agincourt.* The opening of this play gives us a glimpse of the Merry Prince in his madcap days. The first part of *King Henry IV.* was licensed for publication in 1597, the publisher being Andrew Wise. The licence was granted for the publication of " the historye of Henry iiijth. with his battaile of Shrewsbury against Henry Hotspurre of the North with the conceipted mirthe of Sir John Falstaff." The leader of the wild crew with whom Prince Hal associated was at first given the name of " Sir John Oldcastle," and the character was manifestly intended to be a caricature of Sir John Oldcastle, the prominent Lollard leader, who sat in the House of Lords as Lord Cobham, having secured the title by marrying the heiress of a nobleman of that name. Sir John Oldcastle took part in the campaigns against Owain Glyndwr; and as the companion of Henry, Prince of Wales, he became so distinguished for his gaiety and his readiness to humour the Prince's whims that his enemies called him the "ruffian knight, mainly brought in by the commediants on the stage." But Oldcastle was in actual fact very far from being a Falstaff. As the Prince reformed, so did Lord Cobham. He embraced the principles of Lollardism, and Wycliffe had no more stalwart follower. Under a law passed in the reign of Henry IV., Lollards were burned at the stake as heretics, and in the reign of Henry V. Sir John Oldcastle was arrested and sent to the Tower. The King tried to persuade him to recant, but he resolutely refused. He was allowed to escape, and remained for some years hidden among the hills of Vyrnwy in North Wales. He was again arrested in 1417, and in spite of the old friendship of the King was hung alive in chains with a slow fire beneath his feet. As the result of a representation made in high quarters by a descendant of his (Henry Brooke, eighth Lord Cobham, who succeeded to the title in 1596), Shakespeare in his play substituted for the name of Sir John Oldcastle the immortal name of Sir John Falstaff, but he overlooked the reference to the original name in Act I., Scene 2, where Prince Henry refers to him as " my *old* lad of the *Castle*." The only Welsh scene in the play is Scene 1 of Act III., wherein Hotspur, Mortimer, Worcester, and Glendower enter a room in the house of the Archdeacon of Bangor, intending to discuss the "tripartite deed" and map defining the manner in which England and Wales are to be divided between the three leaders. But a compliment paid to Glendower's military valour by Hotspur leads to boasting on Glendower's part: not, indeed, the empty vaunting of a braggart, but the dignified recital of incidents calculated to justify Lancaster's dread of him, which the Northumbrian has commented upon—how his birth was marked and his high destiny foretold by marvellous signs and celestial wonders, among them shooting stars, comets, and earthquakes. Hotspur's reception of these claims is ribald, and a quarrel is narrowly averted, as described in Chapter IX. Glendower leaves the room to fetch the Ladies Percy and Mortimer, that they may take farewell of their husbands; and while he is absent Mortimer and Worcester reprove Hotspur for his mischievous baiting of the Welshman, of whom they both speak in terms of the highest praise. Glendower returning with the Ladies Mortimer and Percy, there follows the scene in which we learn that Mortimer and his bride have no common language but that of passion and affection; and Lady Mortimer, taking her husband's head in her lap, sings " the song that pleaseth " Mortimer—a Welsh song which the poet does not name, nor does tradition tell us what it was.

Glendower, resentful of Percy's sceptical remarks as to his powers of magic, informs them that—

> Those musicians that shall play to you
> Hang in the air a thousand leagues from hence,
> Yet straight they shall be here.

Had he, although in a stranger's house, contrived by a little stage-management to secrete a harp, a viol, an oboe or what not behind the arras or panelling? Magicians have been known to practise such deceptions to maintain their reputations; but Shakespeare makes no such suggestion. Then did he hypnotise his hearers? We have no reason to suppose that Shakespeare knew anything of hypnotism, yet he may well have seen or experienced something of it, for it must have been part of the stock-in-trade of the magicians of the day, though how far they themselves understood its nature we do not know. A perusal of *The Tempest* may be held to suggest that Shakespeare had seen it employed or had himself been hypnotised. Be this as it may, the magical music plays, but the effect upon Percy is disappointing; his only comment is: " Now I perceive the devil understands Welsh. . . . By'r lady, he's a good musician."

Lady Percy refuses to follow Lady Mortimer with an English song, and is taken to task for swearing " like a comfit-maker's wife." And with that the men proceed to seal the deed " and then to horse "—Hotspur all unknowing that his farewell to his wife is for all time; and Worcester that a shameful death awaits him, for Glendower, misled by prophecies and omens, fails to keep his rendezvous on the field of Shrewsbury, and Northumberland is sick, and Henry and his son, Hotspur being slain and his forces crushed, march off as the curtain falls—

Towards Wales,
To fight with Glendower and the Earl of March.

## 2. " MERRY WIVES OF WINDSOR."

The main plot of the *Merry Wives of Windsor* is the presentation of the dilemmas into which Sir John Falstaff is forced through his attempted amours with Mrs. Ford and Mrs. Page. His punishments are as ingenious as they are complete. He is carried out in a basket of dirty clothes and pitched into the River Thames; he is soundly belaboured while trying to escape in the disguise of the fat woman of Brentford; he is pinched and burned in the character of " Herne the Hunter," and his pretensions as a libertine exposed before an unsympathetic audience. There is a sub-plot running through the play, in which the principal figures are Sir Hugh Evans, Justice Shallow, Slender, Dr. Caius, and Mine Host of the Garter; and a love-story, Fenton, Slender's rival, courting and eloping with " sweet Anne Page."

*Act I.*, *Scene* I.—The curtain rises to discover Shallow, Slender, and Evans in front of Page's house. Shallow, that merciless caricature of Sir Thomas Lucy, the self-important and unintelligent county magnate, is complaining of an affront which Falstaff is said to have offered him. His negligible cousin, Slender, to salve his wounded vanity, drags in the family coat of arms. The Shallows, he tells Evans, " may give the dozen white luces in their coat "—an obvious reference to the Lucys. Evans, who appears to be amusing himself by " ragging " the two simpletons, observes that " the dozen white louses do become an old coat well . . . it is a familiar beast to man." He acts the part of Chorus—shrewd, witty, talkative, dryly sarcastic—but he is always itching for promo-

226

tion from the Chorus to a leading part. First he wishes to be made arbitrator in the quarrel betwen Shallow and Sir John; then, Shallow having assured Slender that he may quarter the family coat if he marries, we see the restless Welshman as matchmaker; he bethinks him of Anne Page, an heiress—a likely bride for Slender. The latter knows the young gentlewoman (she is very young, being not yet seventeen), and admits that she has " good gifts." Evans dryly agrees that " seven hundred pounds and possibilities [*i.e.*, expectations] is good gifts."

Page enters; he, too, proffers his " good offices " between Shallow and Falstaff, and Evans hints that Slender has matter for his ear. Shallow is still resentful. " Robert Shallow, esquire, saith he is wronged !"

Falstaff appears with Bardolph, Nym, and Pistol, and Shallow at once accuses him. It is curious to note that Shakespeare has made Falstaff guilty of his own offence. " Knight," says Shallow, " you have beaten my men, killed my deer, and broke open my lodge." As for Slender, he too has " matter in his head " against the knight and his " coney-catching rascals." They have made him drunk and afterwards picked his pocket. Evans— always eager to be in the centre of the stage, and also to have all things ordered in a seemly fashion—suggests that he and Page and mine Host of the Garter shall act as umpires. " I will make a prief of it in my note-book; and we will afterwards 'ork upon the cause." He is offended by Pistol's "affectations." The charge is denied, and the indignant Slender swears that in future he will be drunk ' with those that have the fear of God."

Here Mistress Anne Page enters, a Hebe-like figure, bearing wine, Mistress Ford and Mistress Page following her. Anne, at her father's bidding, carries the wine indoors again, and the company are invited to dinner.

Shallow, Slender, and Evans linger without. Poor Slender is in a sweat of nervous dread. He laments that he has not his " book of Songs and Sonnets " with him. His man, Simple, appears. Has Simple his *Book of Riddles?* It is obvious that he wishes to shine before the heiress; but his wits have need of adventitious aid. Shallow bids him come to dinner. Does he understand that Evans has made " a kind of tender, afar off?" He does; he will be reasonable; he will do as Cousin Shallow says. Evans is impatient. " But can you affection the 'oman ?" He will do his best, to please Cousin Shallow, the head of the family. " If there be no great love in the beginning, yet

heaven may decrease it upon better acquaintance....
If you say *marry her*, I will marry her, that I am
freely dissolved, and dissolutely." Evans is content; this is " a fery discretion answer; save the
faul' is in the 'ort dissolutely "; and Shallow " thinks
his cousin meant well." And with this Anne Page
again appears. Will they not come in to dinner?
Shallow and Evans discreetly comply, leaving
Slender with Anne. Slender, having sent Simple
to wait upon Cousin Shallow, seeks to make an
impression; but also—for he is in an agony of
self-conscious embarrassment—to avoid facing the
company within. He would rather walk; he has
bruised his shin; he doesn't like the smell of meat;
yet, despite his poor appetite, he is a perfect devil
of a fellow; he is not afraid of bears, but has "taken
Sackerson, a famous bear in the Paris gardens,
by the chain." Only when Page appears does he
finally bow to his fate and go to dinner.

When at last the twittering Slender has been
induced to enter the house, the Welshman makes
a brief appearance. Simple is with him, and is
bidden to seek " Doctor Caius' house," where
" dwells one Mistress Quickly, which is in the
manner of his nurse, or his dry nurse, or his cook,
or his laundry, his washer, and his wringer." To
her he is to take a letter, requiring her to further

Slender's suit with Anne Page, for the two are close friends. As for Evans, " I will make an end of my dinner," he says; " there's pippins and cheese to come." To Shakespeare, all Welshmen appear fond of cheese.

In *Scene* 4 the letter is delivered. Mistress Quickly bids Rugby, the Doctor's manservant, to watch for the doctor, for " if he find anybody in the house, here will be an old abusing of God's patience and the King's English." Simple is required to describe his master. " Well, heaven send Anne Page no worse a fortune ! Tell master parson Evans I will do what I can for your master." But Caius returns suddenly: Simple is shut in a closet. The Doctor is sent for to Court—*la grande affaire*. At the last moment he dives into the closet—" dere is some simples in my closet." There is also one Simple . . . Caius calls for his rapier; but Mistress Quickly confesses the truth.

Caius calls for paper. Mistress Quickly is " glad he is so quiet." And while he is writing she confides to Simple that " my master himself is in love with Mistress Anne Page."

The quietness is deceptive. The Welshman's love of having a finger in every pie has led him into hot water. " You jack'nape," says the enraged physician, " give-a dis letter to Sir Hugh; by gar,

it is a challenge; I vill cut his troat in de park:
and I will teach a scurvy jackanape priest to meddle
or make." " I have appointed mine host of de
Jarterre to measure our weapon; by gar, I vill
myself have Anne Page."

In *Act II.*, *Scene* 3, we find Caius and Rugby
waiting in Windsor Park. It is past the hour
of the meeting. Caius is impatient, and in a blood-
thirsty mood. If Rugby will take his rapier,
Caius will show him how he intends to kill the
Welshman. Rugby, who is uneasy at this proposal,
is saved by the appearance of Mine Host, Shallow,
Slender, and Page. Shallow boasts that though
old and a justice of the peace, " if I see a sword out
my finger itches to make one." The jolly Host
sends Page, Shallow, and Slender to Frogmore,
where the misdirected Welshman is waiting. He
himself will bring Caius thither by another way.
He has an infallible inducement: " I will bring
thee where Mistress Anne Page is, at a farm-
house."

*Act III.*, *Scene* 1, reveals Evans, with Simple,
in a field near Frogmore. Simple has looked
everywhere for Caius. Evans is " full of cholers,"
but also of " trempling of mind." " I shall be
glad," he says, " if he have deceived me; how
melancholies I am !" If the enemy comes, how-

231

ever, he shall have a rude reception, "pless my soul!" whereat he falls to singing:

> *To shallow rivers, to whose falls*
> *Melodious birds sing madrigals. . . .*

"Mercy on me; I have a great dispositions to cry!"

But here Simple announces the advent of the enemy. "He's welcome," says Evans, and continues to warble of his "shallow rivers." However, it is not Caius who approaches, but Page, Shallow, and Slender. Does he study the word and the sword? says Shallow. And youthful still, in doublet and hose, this raw rheumatic day? "There is reasons and causes for it," says Evans, with dignity. Slender, since the dinner, is reduced to babbling: "O sweet Anne Page." Evidently he has discovered that "he can affection the 'oman." And here the Host, Caius, and Rugby appear. Evans is quick to read in Mine Host's expansive countenance the fact that a practical joke has been played upon him. He rapidly whispers a conciliatory word or two in the Frenchman's ear, while for the benefit of the company he repeats his previous threats. Mine Host, bubbling over with jollity and good will, confesses his stratagem. Shall he lose his parson and his priest? Never; let them shake hands "and let burnt sack be the issue." And in pursuance of his invitation they all follow to the Garter; but the Welshman and the Frenchman, lingering behind, resolve upon vengeance. They will " knog their brains together."

*Act IV*. opens with the scene wherein Evans puts William through his paces, as described in Chapter I. In *Scene* 4 Page, Ford, their wives, and Evans, discuss the vengeance which is to overtake Falstaff, the suggestion of the two women being that the knight shall be induced to meet them " by Herne's oak " " in deep of night," " disguised like Herne, with great horns on his head," when he is to be surprised by a troop of children dressed as fairies, who will pinch, burn, and upbraid him. Evans will " be like a jack-an-apes also," and will " teach the children their behaviours." In *Scene* 5 the parson and the doctor have their revenge upon Mine Host; having heard of Bardolph's mishap with the " cousin-Germans," they solemnly warn the Host to look well to his horses—" out of good will."

In *Act V.*, *Scene* 3 (*The street in Windsor*), at night Mistress Page and Mistress Ford and Dr. Caius come upon the stage. Mrs. Page has given her consent to a marriage between Caius and her daughter; he is to seize upon the girl in green and " away with her to the deanery." We

learn that the punishment of Falstaff is prepared.
" Where is Nan now," says Mrs. Ford, "and her
troop of fairies ? and the Welch devil, Hugh ?"
"They are all couched in a pit hard by Herne's
oak, with obscured lights," and "the hour
draws on."

In *Scene* 4, in Windsor Park, " Enter Sir
Hugh Evans and Fairies." The " Welch devil's "
opening words tell us that he is master of cere-
monies, as arranged; he has " taught the children
their behaviours." " Trib, trib, fairies, and
remember your parts; be pold, I pray you; follow
me into the pit, and when I give you the watch
'ords do as I pid you; come, come, trib."

In *Scene* 5 the amorous Falstaff, since "the Windsor
bell hath struck twelve," appears in the Park, as
the phantom Herne the hunter—"disguised, with
a buck's head on."

Mistress Ford keeps her tryst; but with her is
Mistress Page. Falstaff is nothing loth. " Divide
me !" he cries. " Cupid makes restitution !" But,
alas ! disillusion is swift. There is a " noise within,"
and Sir Hugh Evans, " like a Satyr," comes upon
the scene with " Anne Page as the Fairy Queen,
attended by her Brother and others, dressed like
Fairies, with waxen tapers on their heads."

One is tempted to quote the whole scene for the

234

sake of the delightful verse, only matched in *A Midsummer Night's Dream*. Anne, Hobgoblin, and the Satyr " make the fairy O-yes "—in other words, they give their attendant fairies their orders for the night. The tasks which are set them are peculiarly characteristic of the Welsh Pwcca, though reminiscent of the Hobgoblin or Brownie of the English and Scottish peasantry. " They are fairies !" cries Falstaff. " No man their works must eye !" And he lies down upon his face.

Before the fairies disperse to their nightly task Evans (who, besides turning poet, has for the nonce lost his Welsh accent) calls them together for their " dance of custom round about the oak of Herne the hunter."

Pray lock you hand in hand: yourselves in order set,
And twenty glow-worms shall our lanterns be,
To guide our measure round about the tree.
But stay ! I smell a man of middle earth !

" Heaven defend me," cries Falstaff, " from that Welsh fairy, lest he transform me to a piece of cheese !" From which we infer that Evans had not, after all, quite lost his accent in becoming a Satyr, although no trace of it appears in the text of the verse.

Evans does not transform Falstaff into his favourite form of nourishment; he treats him as

235

if he were already transformed. Literally and metaphorically, he proceeds to " roast " him. " If he be chaste " the flame of the fairies' tapers will refuse to burn his fingers; if otherwise . . . The night rings with the protest of sinful flesh, and the fairies dance about him, pinching him. But now other mortals appear. Caius, creeping forward, steals away with " a fairy in green "; Slender with " a fairy in white "; and Fenton with the real Anne Page. Then, at a " noise of hunting," the fairies fly; Page, Ford, Mistress Page, and Mistress Ford appear and " lay hold on Falstaff." " I do begin to perceive," he says, after suffering Ford's gibes, " that I am made an ass." " Have I lived to stand at the taunt of one that makes fritters of English ?" But the fat old rascal, after suffering a round of robust Elizabethan abuse, is forgiven: Page bids him " eat a posset " at his house, being in high good humour. " Laugh at my wife that now laughs at thee," he says. " Master Slender hath married her daughter." For he had arranged with Slender to elope with her, as his wife had conspired with Caius. But Mrs. Page is very sure that Anne is by now the wife of the doctor.

Here, however, Slender returns, disconsolate, for his bride is " a great lubberly boy," " a post-master's boy." And Dr. Caius, too, is " cozened " in his turn; he has married " un garcon, a boy, a paysan," and will " raise all Windsor." " Who hath got the right Anne ?" cries Ford.

The mystery is resolved by the advent of Fenton with the " right Anne," whom he has hastily but lawfully wedded. And so, the parents forgiving her and him, the party go homeward to "laugh this sport o'er by a country fire, Sir John and all."

### 3. "KING HENRY V."

The year of the composition of *King Henry V.* (viz., 1599) has been exactly determined by the well-known allusion to Essex in the prologue of Act V. Essex left London to suppress a rebellion in Ireland on March 27th, 1599. He returned to England in disgrace in September of the same year. From the tenor of this prologue, which is anticipatory as well as complimentary, it is concluded that the play was completed and acted between the two dates we have mentioned. The play was first published in quarto in 1600, and its fidelity to history is greater than that of any of Shakespeare's other plays. " The play itself," says Brandes, " is an epic in dialogue. . . . Its theme is English patriotism, and its appeal is to England rather than to the world. It is a national anthem in five acts." It contains a wealth of beautiful

237

imagery and noble rhetoric which raises its poetry to unusual heights.

Fluellen appears in no less than six scenes, and through his intimacy with the King is brought into considerable prominence. The Scotch and Irish captains appear only in one scene—namely, in Scene 2 of Act III. It is suggested that this scene, in which the four captains are brought together, was a later insertion. The compliment which Fluellen pays to the Scotsman, Jamy, is certainly in conflict with the anti-Scottish sentiments expressed in the second scene of the play. The supposition is that this scene did not form part of the original version, but was added after the death of Elizabeth to please her successor, King James, " who had been annoyed that year by depreciation of Scotsmen on the stage." If this assumption be correct, then Shakespeare used Fluellen as the medium for mollifying the King. " The character of Fluellen," says Gervinus, " should be exhibited by the Actor as it was by Hippisley in Garrick's time, without playfulness or caricature."

In *Act III., Scene 2*, the British forces are before Harfleur. Nym, Bardolph, Pistol, and a Boy are on the stage, Bardolph seeking to drive them to a breach in the French works. But the others demur; " the humour of it is too hot."

238

To them enters Fluellen, who wastes no words. "Got's plood! Up to the preaches, you rascals! will you not up to the preaches?" And "up to the preaches" he drives them, protesting: all but the Boy, who, as "boy to all three" of the "swashers," entertains the audience with his shrewd Cockney comments upon them.

Fluellen re-enters with Gower, and the scene with the Scottish and Irish captains follows. Macmorris is unwilling to oblige Fluellen and Jamy by "voutsafing a few disputations, look you, as partly touching or concerning the disciplines of the war," and takes such offence at a reference to his "nation" that he and the valiant Welshman are on the verge of a quarrel, when "the town sounds a parley."

In *Act III.*, *Scene* 6, the English are in camp in Picardy. Again there is an action in progress near by; Gower, meeting Fluellen, hails him with the query: "Come you from the bridge?" Fluellen does come from the bridge, and "there is very excellent service committed at the bridge," and "the Duke of Exeter is as magnanimous as Agamemnon," while "an aunchient" is "as valiant as Mark Antony."

It is to be noted that all three of Shakespeare's chief Welsh characters are diligent readers and students. Evans, perhaps, is rather a grammarian than a lover of letters; but Glendower is widely read in many branches of knowledge, a student of the occult, of ancient Welsh literature, and of music, and is himself a poet and musician; while Fluellen has his Homer and Plutarch and Virgil at his fingers' ends, and is deeply versed in military history and biography and the literature of war. In this Shakespeare, as usual, is true to life. The Welsh have always been great readers; if they have not figured much in English letters, it is perhaps because they have paid more attention to their own language and to the classics.

It appears that the ancient who has performed such prodigies of valour at the bridge is one Pistol. Gower denies knowledge of him. And here Pistol enters, to beg Fluellen's intercession with the Duke of Exeter for the life of Bardolph, who has stolen a pyx and is condemned to die " a damned death." Fluellen refuses, " for disciplines ought to be used "; and Ancient Pistol departs with a " Die and be damned !"

The Pistolian jargon has jogged Gower's memory. "Why, this is an arrant counterfeit rascal; I remember him now; a bawd; a cutpurse." Fluellen's reply reveals the lovable simplicity of a brave and truthful man who is not overburdened with a

240

sense of humour. "I'll assure you 'a uttered as prave 'ords at the pridge as you shall see in a summer's day," he says; whereupon Gower enlightens him: "A gull, a fool, a rogue, that now and then goes to the wars, to grace himself, at his return to London, under the form of a soldier. . . . And what a beard of the general's cut, and a horrid suit of the camp, will do among foaming bottles and ale-washed wits, is wonderful to be thought on; but you must learn to know such slanders of the age."

Now the King enters with Gloster. Henry, on hearing that Fluellen comes from the bridge, asks for a report of the action; he learns that "the perdition of th' athversary hath been very reasonable great; marry, for my part I think the duke hath lost never a man but one that is like to be executed for robbing a church." Henry renews his orders that there is to be no looting, no ill-treatment of the French—an act of policy as much as of humanity, "for when lenity and cruelty play for a kingdom the gentler gamester is the soonest winner."

In *Act IV., Scene* 1, we have the meeting between Pistol and the King, in which the King declares himself a Welshman; whereon Pistol bids him tell Fluellen—since this unknown Welshman confesses to knowing him—that he'll " knock his leek about his pate upon St. Davy's day." And if the stranger is Fluellen's friend " the *figo* for him." Whereat the Ancient departs, remarking that his name is Pistol—a name, as the King observes, which " sorts well with his fierceness."

Here Gower and Fluellen " enter severally." Gower calls to Fluellen, and is taken to task for speaking loudly in the neighbourhood of the enemy. " It is the greatest admiration in the universal 'orld when the true and ancient prerogatifes and laws of the wars is not kept; if you would take the pains but to examine the wars of Pompey the Great, you shall find, I warrant you, that there is no tiddle-taddle or pibble-pabble in Pompey's camp." And on Gower objecting that " the enemy is loud; you heard him all night," he replies scathingly: " If the enemy is an ass, and a fool, and a prating coxcomb, is it meet, think you, that we should also, look you, be an ass, and a fool, and a prating coxcomb, in your conscience now ? To which Gower sensibly replies that he " will speak lower." And Henry, who has been an unobserved witness, remarks:

> Though it appear a little out of fashion,
> There is much care and valour in this Welshman.

In *Scene 7* of the same act Fluellen and Gower enter amid " alarums." Fluellen is in a heat of righteous indignation; a crime has been committed. " Kill the poys and the luggage!" he exclaims; " 'tis expressly against the law of arms !" It is said that reprisals have been taken. " 'Tis certain there's not a boy left alive . . . wherefore the king most worthily hath caused every soldier to cut his prisoner's throat." Reprisals in those days did not take the form of Governmental " notes." The morality of vicarious punishment may seem a little doubtful to us, but it is plain that Gower admires it. " O, 'tis a gallant king !" It is here that Fluellen, as we saw in Chapter XII., makes his famous comparison between King Henry and Alexander. Not only was one born at Monmouth and one in Macedon; not only is there a river in both places; but Alexander "in his rages, and his furies, and his wraths, and his cholers, and his moods, and his displeasures, and his indignations, did, in his ales and his angers, kill his pest friend."

"Our king is not like him in that," cries Gower: " he never killed any of his friends."

Here Fluellen betrays the true touchiness of the Welshman, who does not gladly suffer contradiction. " It is not well done, mark you now, to take the tales out of my mouth ere it is made an end and finished. I speak but in the figures and comparisons of it: As Alexander is kill his friend Cleitus, being in his ales and his cups, so also Harry Monmouth, being in his right wits and his goot judgments, is turn away the fat knight with the great pelly-doublet . . . I forget his name. . . . I can tell you, there is goot men porn at Monmouth." All of which amounts to this: Alexander, drunk, killed his friend; Henry, sober, turned his friend away. One was born in Macedon, one at Monmouth, and there is an *m* and a river in each. It would be difficult to find a better example of the curious Welshman's faculty of seeing what he desires or fears to see in obscure prophecies or omens —the very weakness that lost Glendower the Battle of Shrewsbury and a throne, and probably cost his chief accomplices their lives.

Now enters Henry in a royal rage, " with part of the English forces," accompanied by Warwick, Gloster, Exeter, and others. We may suppose his anger to be due to the killing of the " poys " and the looting of all his luggage. Catching sight of a body of horsemen upon a hill, he bids a herald ride up to them.

> If they will fight with us bid them come down
> Or void the field. . . .
> If they'll do neither we will come to them
> And make them skirr away. . . .

> Besides, we'll cut the throats of those we have,
> And not a man of them that we shall take
> Shall taste our mercy. . . .

From which we gather that the reprisals on the killing of the camp servants have not yet been taken. But here a French herald appears with crestfallen bearing; his errand is to beg an armistice that the French may gather up the dead and wounded; " for many of our princes—woe the while !—lie drown'd and soak'd in mercenary blood." Henry is doubtful; he is not even sure that he has won the day. The herald is in no such doubt. " The day is yours," he confesses. " Praised be God, and not our strength for it !" cries Henry. " What is this castle call'd that stands hard by ?". " They call it Agincourt." "Then we call this the field of Agincourt."

And here Fluellen is ready with his knowledge of the " histories of the wars." On this very ground, he says, Henry's grandfather (he means his great-grandfather) and his great-uncle the Black Prince fought an action, in which the Welsh " did goot service in a garden where leeks did grow, wearing leeks in their Monmouth caps," that they might be known from the enemy; wherefore the leek is " an honourable padge of the service " (a commemorative emblem of the occasion), and

245

even the King now wears the leek "upon St. Tavy's day." The King agrees; " for I am Welsh, you know, good countryman." And Fluellen, remembering his assertion that " there is goot men porn in Monmouth," exclaims, in a burst of enthusiastic patriotism and loyalty, " All the water in Wye cannot wash your majesty's Welsh plood out of your pody."

Then follows the scene wherein Fluellen is appealed to as an expert on the point of honour. Henry has caught sight of Williams, with whom he exchanged gloves as a gage of the quarrel between them. " Soldier," he says, " why wears't thou that glove in thy cap ?" Williams explains. But what, says Henry, if the " rascal that swaggered " is " a gentleman of great sort ?" " Though he be as good a gentleman as the devil is . . . it is necessary, look you, that he keep his vow and oath," is Fluellen's reply. So the soldier is dismissed with an admonition to keep his vow; and Henry gives Fluellen the glove which he had of Williams. It was plucked from Alençon's helm, says Henry; let Fluellen wear it; if any man challenge it " he is a friend to Alençon," and to be apprehended as an enemy.

Fluellen is delighted at the prospect of a quarrel " according to the disciplines of war," and is despatched, as Williams was, to summon Gower. Having thus insured that Williams and Fluellen shall meet and perceive one another's gages of battle, Henry requests Warwick and Gloster to follow Fluellen and " see there be no harm between them "; for it has just struck him that his love of practical joking may result in mischief, since Fluellen is "hot as gunpowder, and quickly will return an injury." Having taken which precaution, he leaves the stage with Exeter.

In *Scene* 8 we find Williams returning with Gower, who has evidently been wondering why Henry wants him. Williams " warrants it is to knight him." And now Fluellen overtakes him with the same message as Williams; he, too, thinks honours are in store for Gower. But he has no time to say more: Williams' challenge is immediate at the sight of his glove, and the challenge is accompanied by a blow. " 'S blood !" cries Fluellen, horrified to find a friend of Alençon's in the person of an English soldier and the company of the loyal Gower; " an arrant traitor as any's in the universal 'orld, or in France, or in England !" and apprehends him in the King's name. Fortunately Warwick and Gloster, followed by Henry, with Exeter, are in time to prevent mischief; and the " most contagious treason " is explained.

247

Williams makes a sturdy but respectful defence and is dismissed with the glove full of crowns, with permission to wear it " as an honour." Fluellen, not to seem ungenerous, for " the fellow has mettle enough in his belly," offers him an additional twelve pence. " Hold, there is twelve pence for you, and I pray you to serve God, and keep you out of prawls and prabbles and quarrels and dissensions."

Williams, as touchy in his way as the Welshman, feels that he is being patronised, and refuses the money; whereupon Fluellen, with the curious practical obtuseness and simplicity which prevents him from understanding the sensitiveness of another man, presses it upon him. " It is with a goot will . . it will serve you to mend your shoes: come, wherefore should you be so pashful ? your shoes are not so goot: 'tis a good silling . . . or I will change it."

In *Act V.*, *Scene* 1, we have the famous encounter between Pistol and Fluellen, wherein the " turkey-cock," the " beggarly, pragging knave," is compelled, by the wrathful Welshman, to eat the leek— an incident fully commented upon in Chapter XII. It reveals a man of great self-control, despite his fire-eating propensities; able to measure his revenge by the measure of his will; not carried away by his anger, but disciplined even in his wrath. And with this scene as a fitting climax—a scene which, as we have suggested, may have been devised to put an end to English ridicule of the Welsh—we take our leave of this notable character.

# CONCLUSIONS

It is impossible to consider Shakespeare's Welshmen as fully as we have done in the foregoing
pages without realising that the poet had made a
close and careful study of the Welsh character.
His allusions to Welsh traditions and beliefs prove
that he knew at least something of Welsh literature.
His fairy poetry gives us reason to believe that he
was at least moderately familiar with Welsh folklore. There remains the question, Did he ever
travel in Wales? To which we may reply, Why
not? Stratford is only fifty miles from the border
of Monmouthshire, which in his days was reckoned
part of Wales, and sixty from the Welsh border
as we know it, while Herefordshire was but a day's
walk distant. Is it likely that an active boy,
with the love of adventure and the insatiable
curiosity of genius in his veins, had never gone so
far afield? As the son of a prosperous trader,
too, it is likely enough that he went on journeys
with or for his father. Welsh drovers were continually coming to Stratford and returning; there
was a weekly market in the town, and five yearly
fairs, four of which were for cattle. Welsh
farmers and gentlemen, singly and in parties, must
continually have ridden in from Wales. John
Shakespeare, as fellmonger, wool-stapler, glove-

maker, and butcher, would have had business with many of these, and it would be strange if the young Shakespeare had not made many journeys as his father's agent.

At the same time, there is no absolute proof of such journeying, nor can we argue that Shakespeare's knowledge of Wales and the Welsh may be held to afford a proof. On those lines we might argue that he must have travelled in Italy; for his knowledge of Italy and things Italian is singularly accurate, as Sir Edward Sullivan has recently shown us.* As well argue, with the Baconians, that he must have been a courtier, a diplomatist, a soldier, because of his knowledge of affairs. As we have asked elsewhere, What, on these lines, would a future commentator make of the works of Mr. Rudyard Kipling? We need postulate no more than the assimilative powers of genius; we have reasonable proof that Shakespeare had a Welsh grandmother, Welsh cousins, and Welsh friends; moreover, there was what we may fairly call a small Welsh colony in the town in which he grew to manhood. So, if our study of the poet's Welsh characters and Welsh allusions cannot add anything of importance to our knowledge of his life, it will at least convince us that he had many opportunities of observing Welshmen, and we may take his Welsh characters and allusions as the expression of his considered opinion of the Welsh people.

* See *The Nineteenth Century and After*, January and February, 1918, " Shakespeare and Italy."

# INDEX

252

# INDEX

# INDEX

BILLING AND SONS, LIMITED, PRINTERS, GUILDFORD, ENGLAND

Lightning Source UK Ltd.
Milton Keynes UK
UKHW011819080819
347642UK00001B/104/P